JOHN ADAMS

ENCYCLOPEDIA of PRESIDENTS

John Adams

Second President of the United States

By Marlene Targ Brill

CHILDRENS PRESS®
CHICAGO

The Adams mansion in Quincy, Massachusetts

Library of Congress Cataloging-in-Publication Data

Brill, Marlene Targ.
  John Adams.

  (Encyclopedia of presidents)
  Includes index.
  Summary: A biography of the outspoken, decisive
man who served the United States in many ways,
including as its President.
  1. Adams, John, 1735-1826—Juvenile literature.
2. Presidents—United States—Biography—Juvenile
literature. [1. Adams, John, 1735-1826.
2. Presidents] I. Title. II. Series.
E322.B797   1986   973.4'4   [92]   86-13636
ISBN 0-516-01384-X

Picture Acknowledgments

The Bettmann Archive—9, 11, 24 (2 photos), 42
(top), 43 (bottom), 57 (2 photos), 65, 68, 79, 81,
83, 85
Historical Pictures Service—37, 44, 74 (bottom)
Library of Congress—12 (bottom), 13 (top left),
20, 52, 58, 62, 64, 66, 72 (right)
National Park Service, U.S. Department of the
Interior: Abbie Rowe—89
Nawrocki Stock Photo:
© William S. Nawrocki—5
North Wind Picture Archives—4, 6, 13 (bottom
2 photos), 16, 17, 19, 21, 23, 26, 28, 35
(2 photos), 36, 39, 41, 42 (bottom), 46
(3 photos), 49, 50 (2 photos), 51, 53, 54
(2 photos), 56, 60, 61, 63, 67, 71, 72 (left and
center), 74 (top), 77, 78, 82, 86, 88 (top)
Quincy Historical Society: Mrs. Rudolph O.
Oberg—12 (top), 14 (2 photos), 32 (top)
H. Armstrong Roberts—32 (bottom), 43 (top)
Roloc Color Slides—76
U.S. Bureau of Printing and Engraving—2, 13
(top right), 88 (left and center)

Cover design and illustration by
Steven Gaston Dobson

John Adams appears on this three-inch bronze Indian peace medal (shown larger than actual size here). The medal was given to a tribal chief in 1797 as a token of a peace treaty between the United States and his tribe.

Table of Contents

John Adams

Chapter 1

Paying the Price of Peace

John Adams, the second president of the United States, rose to address a special session of Congress. He had just taken office on March 4, 1797, and George Washington had left him with a nation in turmoil. England and France were at war, but neither wanted to recognize the infant nation of America. Although both countries repeatedly insulted the United States, France posed the greater threat.

The French refused to receive American peace agents. Worse yet, France had issued a decree to seize United States ships and cargo. Any American seamen found on ships captured by the British were to be hanged. In response to these assaults, President Adams pressed for a navy, more funds for the military, and a mission of three men to negotiate peace with France.

Reactions to his speech were as divided as the two emerging political parties. Federalists, who believed in a strong central government and sided with England, wanted war with France. They applauded the president for his firm stand on United States dignity. But the Republicans, who supported rule by the people and sided with France, condemned any unnecessary attack on the French.

Adams had tried to keep the country neutral and peaceful. He balanced the people's feelings for and against France and England. Privately, he trusted neither country. Nevertheless, the problem with France was growing into one of the most difficult issues of his presidency.

Now, at age sixty-one, John Adams could look back on a life devoted to his country. His religious background had given him a strong sense of duty. Even as a young lawyer he had written, "The only principles of public conduct that are worthy a gentleman . . . are to sacrifice estate, ease, health, and applause, and even life itself to the sacred calls of his country."

But Adams always felt that others stood in the way of his high ideals. As he often took unpopular stands, he was frequently an unpopular public figure. His every move was questioned. Many people respected the short, stout man for his education, courage, and patriotism. But many more found him too independent, outspoken, and quarrelsome.

Benjamin Franklin once said that Adams "means well for his country, is always an honest man, often a wise one, but sometimes and in some things absolutely out of his senses."

This 1798 cartoon shows a brawl in Congress between
Federalist Roger Griswold and Republican Matthew Lyon.

However, Adams always gave his best for democracy.
Only months earlier, the election of Adams as Federalist
party president and Thomas Jefferson as Republican party
vice-president had been hailed by both parties. One
official remarked of their victory, "I hope that in a short
time, we shall have no interests or views but what are
purely American."

The excitement of the election was short-lived. In Congress, the House and Senate haggled for months while
Adams waited for an answer to his proposals concerning

France. Northern merchants demanded protection for their merchant ships. Southern farmers saw no reason for an expensive navy to protect northern ships. Debate became heated. While Federalists threatened to pull away from the country, Republicans warned of civil war.

Throughout the United States, passions ran high. Citizens crossed the street to avoid tipping their hats to neighbors who took different political sides. Thomas Jefferson and John Adams locked horns openly. Adams called his old friend "weak, uninformed, and ignorant." Jefferson privately told the French consul general that Adams was "obstinate, excessively vain, and takes no counsel from anyone."

Adams and the United States were faced with intrigue on both sides of the Atlantic. In the scandal known as the XYZ Affair, the French said they would receive American peace ministers only if the United States paid a $250,000 bribe and loaned France $12 million.

At home, Adams's cabinet members—most of them appointed by George Washington—secretly plotted behind his back to control the government. They undermined his authority at every turn.

Throughout these difficulties, Adams persisted in his quest for peace. When Americans discovered the proposed bribery, there was a ground swell of public opinion against the French. "Millions for defense but not one cent for tribute" became the slogan of the day. Adams finally won his requests for harbor defenses, a national militia, and a navy to protect merchant ships. Then he asked his cabinet to vote on proclaiming war.

This political cartoon on the XYZ Affair shows France as a monster demanding money from America.

About that time, the French sent word that they would receive United States ministers in proper diplomatic fashion. Against all cabinet cries for war, Adams ordered three ministers to France. What followed was the peace Adams had dreamed of. Over much opposition, he had led the country safely through its infancy. The United States could now stand proud among other nations of the world.

Peace with France cost Adams his party standing. The Federalist party crumbled during the next election. And Adams lost one of his closest allies, Thomas Jefferson.

But to Adams, peace was the high point in his career. "If there is one statement I would like on my tombstone," he wrote, "it would be, 'He made peace with France.'" How fortunate for America that John Adams had the courage to stand for what he believed to be right.

Rooms in the Adamses' cottage: the birth room (above) and the kitchen (below)

Left: Abigail Adams, John's wife. Her letters and memoirs reveal much about life and politics of the time.
Above: John Quincy Adams, John and Abigail's son, became the sixth president of the United States.
Below: Charles Francis Adams, John Quincy Adams's son, was a great American diplomat of the 1860s.
Below left: Samuel Adams, John Adams's cousin, was a leader in the American revolutionary movement.

Chapter 2

Life in Braintree

Young John Adams learned to speak his mind early in life. His father had his heart set on John's going to college. But John only wanted to farm his father's land. Almost all the men in the colonies farmed, so why couldn't he?

John loved his father's farm in Braintree, Massachusetts, one of the several hundred small farms dotting the coastal road between Boston and Plymouth. He had lived there since he was born on October 30, 1735. He especially liked the pleasant smells of wild salt hay and the nearby sea. He knew every inch of land, from the rocky pastures where sheep grazed to the fields of wheat and barley to the surrounding forest and swamp.

John also knew that farming was hard work, but he didn't mind. Although stocky, by the age of fourteen John had strong, broad shoulders and could handle a heavier work load than any other boy in Braintree, with energy left for fishing and hunting. Even as children, he and his younger brothers, Peter and Elihu, helped their parents carry water from the well, chop wood for heat and cooking, milk the cows, and clean the animal stalls.

Opposite: John Adams's birthplace (top) and the original kitchen of his Quincy home (bottom)

A 1739 print of Harvard College, America's oldest university

Nonetheless, the elder John Adams wanted his son John to go to Harvard College and study for the ministry as John's older brother had done. According to the usual custom in the mid-eighteenth century, the oldest son received an education while the other boys inherited larger portions of land. But Mr. Adams wanted more than that for his son John.

The Adams family was a pious family, as were their New England neighbors. John's father was descended from a long line of devout Puritans who were farmers and tradesmen. Henry Adams, John's great-great-grandfather, was one of a group of Puritans who came to America in 1638. He left his farm in England for Massachusetts to seek religious freedom and to escape persecution.

The Puritan meeting house in Hingham, Massachusetts, a few miles from Braintree

Puritans believed in a very strict form of Christianity. They were simple people with plain tastes. Other people's religious views and many modern comforts were considered sinful. But once they were free to practice their faith without interference in America, many Puritans became as intolerant of others as the English had been of them.

Some of John's earliest recollections were of Sundays in church with his family. Each Sunday the entire town met for two church services, one in the morning and one in the afternoon. School was closed and there was no work or play. Except for people going to and from church, the streets were empty.

Church service consisted mainly of a lengthy sermon reminding people of their sins and urging them to change their lives through good deeds. The rest of the service was devoted to the unaccompanied singing of psalms. Organs and other musical instruments were thought to be sinful.

John didn't mind sitting in the gallery with the other boys, the Negroes, and the Indians. He was proud to watch his parents in their place of honor among the grown-ups. A family's place in church depended on their standing within the town.

Although John's father had little education or wealth, he was church deacon and town tax collector, constable, shoemaker, and militia officer. As a respected man in town and a church officer, he sat next to the minister in front of the pulpit.

During the two-hour service John and his brothers fidgeted to keep warm on the hard wooden benches. Since there was no fire in the church, the Adamses and their neighbors brought foot stoves with hot coals to warm their toes. On several occasions the church was so cold that the Communion bread froze on the plate. Everyone who lasted through the day felt stronger in spirit for the experience.

Between the two Sunday services, people visited neighbors, the nearby inn, or the horse shed by the church for a midday cold meal and a warm fire. Women shared stories, recipes, and quilting patterns, while the men talked about crops, cattle prices, and town meetings. John liked to join the men for discussion. He enjoyed talking so much that his Uncle Peter called him the "talkingest boy" he ever knew.

Townspeople got a chance to speak their minds
at New England town meetings.

John inherited this trait—along with a quick tongue—
from his mother, Susanna. Susanna Boylston Adams was as
emotional and industrious as she was talkative. Like his
mother, John earned a reputation for being decisive yet
hot-tempered.

Susanna came from a well-educated family. Her father
was the physician who first introduced the smallpox vac-
cination to the British Empire. Many people hinted that
Deacon Adams raised his social and economic status by
marrying the daughter of such a cultured and prominent
Massachusetts family.

A typical New England kitchen in the 1700s

Although Deacon Adams had little learning, both he and his wife shared a desire for their sons to have a good education. John learned to read while very young. In the modest, two-story clapboard house where he grew up, his father drilled him on the alphabet as they sat by the fire.

Later John joined other children of Braintree in the one-room schoolhouse where they were taught by Mrs. Belcher, a neighbor. Here he studied reading, writing, and arithmetic—his favorite subject—all taught with strong moral overtones.

John liked his early schooling. Mrs. Belcher was stern but kind to the sensitive boy. John did so well with her that he dreaded moving up to the public Latin school taught by Joseph Cleverly.

A schoolhouse in colonial times

Mr. Cleverly was a bored bachelor who lacked enthusiasm for teaching. Each day he made the boys recite from *Lily's Latin Grammar* and from the *Westminster Catechism.*

John soon became bored with school, too. He resented Mr. Cleverly's teaching methods, and he hated studying nothing but Latin grammar.

John started skipping school. He would sneak off to the beaches and muddy marshes to play. As he wrote later, "I spent my time as idle Children do in making and sailing boats and Ships upon the Ponds and Brooks, in making and flying Kites, in driving hoops, playing marbles, playing Quoits, Wrestling, Swimming, Skating, and above all in shooting, to which Diversion I was addicted."

When his father heard of John's misadventures, he scolded the ten-year-old for wasting his chance for an education. John responded that he did not want to go to college but wanted to farm instead. Deacon Adams then offered to show John what farming *really* was like.

The next day John worked by his father's side from morning to sundown. At the end of the grueling day, Deacon Adams asked his tired and muddy son if he still wanted to be a farmer. John stood firm in his decision. However, his clever father, hoping to shame John into wanting his schooling, said, "When a fool has a prize in his hands, he has no heart to improve it."

Not wanting to appear the fool, John returned to school, only to be bored again. This time he decided to teach himself arithmetic and avoid Latin. He passed his days in school motivated by his defiance of Mr. Cleverly.

By the time John was fourteen, it was clear to Deacon Adams that John would not be ready for Harvard. Again, John implored his father to let him farm. When his father looked disappointed, John asked to be tutored by Mr. Marsh in his private school instead. Mr. Marsh not only enjoyed teaching, but he believed *Lily's Latin Grammar* ought to be burned.

Since Deacon Adams very much wanted his son to go to college, he went to Mr. Marsh the next day. With Mr. Marsh's interest and patience, John applied himself to math, Greek, and even Latin as never before. Not long after John's acceptance at Mr. Marsh's, John's father saw in the boy a reduced interest in hunting fowl and squirrels and an increased appetite for books.

Harvard College in Cambridge, Massachusetts, was founded in 1636.
It was named after John Harvard, who donated money to build it.

Within a year, Mr. Marsh pronounced John ready to take the entrance exams for Harvard College. At age fifteen, a worried John Adams set off for Cambridge, Massachusetts, to take the rigorous tests. He passed, later saying, "I was as light when I came home as I had been heavy when I went; my Master was well pleased and my parents very happy."

Many necessary activities were made into entertaining social events.
Above: A quilting bee. Below: A cornhusking

Chapter 3

Career Bound

Two months before John's sixteenth birthday, he and his father left for Cambridge in the family cart. His father had sold thirty acres of land to pay for John's college tuition and board. John knew he had to do well. With his last glimpse of Braintree, now a thriving community of fifteen hundred people, John wondered how he would manage.

Certainly, he would miss his family and neighbors. He would also miss the good times they had — the sleigh rides and skating in the winter and the huskings, harvesting bees, sheepshearings, and roof raisings in the fall. He could still smell the sweet doughnuts and sponge cake his mother spread in the kitchen for her quilting and spinning bees. Even more, John would miss going with his father to the town meetings every spring and fall. John enjoyed the debates and looked forward to the day when he could take part in making decisions for the town along with his father and other town leaders. Even as a teenager he shared his father's sense of duty to government and country.

Although discipline was strict at Harvard, students managed to group together for informal social gatherings. This picture shows a scene from Harvard student life in 1676.

Life at Harvard was much different from life in Braintree. Founded in 1636, Harvard was the oldest college in America. John Harvard, a Puritan minister, had donated his library and half of his estate to the college, and Puritan church officials ran it.

Although now the school claimed to give a liberal education, John still found it had a religious emphasis. Besides religion, John studied Latin, science, and mathematics. There were no courses leading to professions such as law or medicine. Graduates wishing to enter a profession had to spend two or three years learning their trade from an experienced member of that field.

John lived in a college dormitory that was one of three red brick school buildings around a center court. Each student was assigned to a tutor who was responsible for his behavior and classwork for the four years of study.

Discipline at Harvard was strict. There were penalties for any folly. A person who told a lie, drank, broke the Sabbath, swore, played cards, kept a gun, or went skating without permission had to pay a fine of ten shillings for each offense.

The ninety young men were up by five o'clock, at chapel for prayers by six, and at breakfast by seven. Classes began at eight. Afternoons were for study. There was some free time after six o'clock supper. However, when the curfew bell rang, candles were snuffed and fires put out. No one was allowed off the grounds unless he had good cause and permission from his tutor. Although Boston was a penny ferry ride away, John rarely had reason to go there during his first year.

Despite all the rules, John soon grew to love his studies. Though he was studying for the ministry, Harvard opened his mind to the worldly wonders of learning. His favorite times were spent in the school library, where he could read any of the 3,500 books on the shelves.

With a renewed curiosity for study, John began to question whether or not he should pursue life as a minister. He had gnawing doubts about some of the church doctrines. He still believed in strict observance of the Bible teachings, but he felt that ministers offered their congregations too narrow a view of religion. How could he preach ideas he did not accept?

As commencement neared, John discussed his dilemma with Professor Winthrop, his science teacher. Winthrop suggested teaching for a year or two until he decided what to do. Now all John needed was a job.

Barnabas Hedge, a member of Harvard's class of 1783, wore this suit to his graduation ceremony.

On graduation day, the entire Adams family and many other residents of Braintree traveled to Cambridge to celebrate with John. The program ranked him fifteenth in his class of twenty-four in terms of wealth and social status. But John was proud to be one of the first three in his class for scholarship. With this fine record the Reverend Thaddeus Maccarty, who had been sent by his town council to find a Harvard graduate, offered him a position as schoolmaster at a new grammar school in Worcester, Massachusetts.

Three weeks after graduation in 1755, John—not quite twenty years old yet—made the sixty-mile trip to Worcester on horseback. Worcester, a town about the same size as Braintree, was more self-sufficient. Without a post office or stagecoach, the people of Worcester relied less on Boston or London for supplies and news than did the people of Braintree.

John stayed with Mr. Maccarty while he taught Latin to the children in Maccarty's congregation for a small salary. Other friendly residents of Worcester invited the bright Harvard graduate to dine and join them in local chatter.

Talk in Worcester was more political than in John's hometown. Worcester was in the center of the Massachusetts colony, and since it was the county seat many lawyers lived there.

Discussion usually centered around England and France. The two had been fighting for almost fifty years over land borders within America, fishing rights, and control of trade with the Indians. Because the English settlers farmed on Indian hunting grounds, the Indians sided with the French. Only seven years earlier the Nipmucks had raided Worcester, so relations between the French and Indians was an important topic.

By 1754, the French had claimed Canada and were moving south into the Ohio Valley. There they built Fort Duquesne after pushing back George Washington's Virginia troops. After the French captured Fort William Henry, New Englanders feared the capture of Fort Edward and then of all of Massachusetts. When the French did not advance, people in Massachusetts were relieved.

John listened to the talk of politics but contributed little. Privately, he wondered whether power in the colonies would ever transfer from England and France to America. However, his main interest was in choosing a profession.

Although the people of Worcester were kind to him, John was terribly homesick and unhappy. He knew he couldn't stay in Worcester the rest of his life. And after a short time, it was painfully clear that teaching was not for him. To escape, John threw himself into his studies and began writing a diary.

John taught all the boys from the town and countryside between the ages of five and fifteen. The barren, one-room schoolhouse was much like the one he remembered at Mr. Cleverly's. Unfortunately, the daily routine he prescribed for his fifty charges was likewise similar. As he wrote in his diary, "Every week day is a sacrifice. . . . I am certain that teaching . . . any length of time would make a base weed . . . of me."

Life in the colonies at this time was becoming more secular. Increasingly, when people wanted money and power, they turned to business—shipping, lumber, fishing, land speculation—rather than to the church. John wanted to make his mark in the world, too. But his family had neither the money nor the influence to set him up in business. Over his parents' protests, John looked to law as a career.

In earlier times, many religious groups believed that lawyers were doing the work of the devil and that the laws of God should overrule the laws of man. In 1730, the colony of Rhode Island passed a law barring lawyers from holding political office. That same year, the New York colony allowed only eight lawyers in the courts.

But the French and Indian Wars and a growing trade with England created a need for lawyers. There were army contracts, smuggling, and all forms of business investments to be handled. By the mid-1700s, lawyers began to be respected.

In larger towns like Boston, lawyers were becoming professional politicians. People selected them as town officers. Since the thirteen colonies together had a population about the same size as London's, a successful lawyer in Boston could make a name for himself. John decided to teach until he had enough money to study law and start a practice in Boston.

After one year as schoolmaster, John asked James Putnam, a successful Worcester lawyer, to take him into his office to learn law. For the next two years John lived with Putnam while he copied deeds and wills, studied law, prepared briefs, and discussed court cases. During the day he labored at Worcester Latin School, making lessons as interesting as he could. He became so busy he had no time even to write in his diary.

By October 1, 1758, the noted Boston lawyers Jeremiah Gridley and James Otis introduced John into legal practice in Boston. As John headed home to Braintree, he thought of two pieces of advice from Gridley:

"One is to pursue Study of the Law, rather than the gain of it. . . . The next is, not to marry early, for an early Marriage will obstruct your Improvement, and . . . will involve you in Expence."

Above: John Adams's law office, in his home, used to be the kitchen. Here he, Samuel Adams, and James Bowdoin worked on the Massachusetts state constitution.
Below: Boston, where Adams did much of his law work

Chapter 4

The Young Lawyer

Back in Braintree, John opened his law practice in the parlor of the family farm. As the city was too small to keep a single lawyer occupied with work, he had few cases to bring in fees. Although he was considered a bright young lawyer, John doubted whether he would ever achieve the greatness he desired.

To attract business, John rode to nearby towns to meet judges and sheriffs who might know of someone needing a competent lawyer. To learn more law he watched court proceedings in Boston, where he began to make important acquaintances.

At home, John studied civil law and attended town meetings as he had done when he was a boy. Only now he took part in the discussions along with his father.

Early in 1761 John was nominated for surveyor of the highways for the township and later was chosen to be a selectman, or city council member. Although town offices offered no pay, he was eager to serve the public and performed his duties with his usual vigor.

Life was not all law for John. At night he played cards or backgammon, read aloud, and smoked tobacco with friends. Whenever he had time he went home with other men to discuss world events and court the ladies.

Remembering Gridley's warning, he had no intention of marrying. But he did enjoy the company of a lady named Hannah Quincy. According to John, Hannah was a flirt, but she "thinks more than most of her Sex."

The etiquette of the day saved John from losing himself to Hannah. They were never left alone for long, even when strolling in Cupid's Grove, the lovers' lane of Braintree. The one time Hannah and John were alone, he almost proposed. When her brother came in unexpectedly, John came to his senses, left the room, and never returned.

John passed the empty days by concentrating on his books. His scholarly pursuits were gaining him the respect of some of Boston's well-known lawyers. More and more frequently, he made the ten-mile trip to Boston to handle his growing practice.

In 1761, John attended a trial that would affect him the rest of his life. The trial came about because of local opposition to England's strict rules of trade.

Just one year before, England had won its war with France. French troops left North America for the first time in almost seventy years, and all America celebrated. John and his neighbors applauded the news with a day of prayer and fasting.

However, the celebration was short-lived. King George III felt that England was losing money by not requiring all of America's trade to pass through the mother country.

Great Britain's King George III (right) wished to profit from America's trade by charging import taxes. American merchant ships (below) were bringing in goods from many distant ports.

American merchants were prospering from direct trade with the French West Indies, Spain, and Dutch-owned islands. England wanted some profit from this trade to pay its staggering war debt and to keep a peacetime military to protect its empire.

So England firmly restricted American trade and ordered tariffs, or taxes, on all products bought and sold. Boston merchants believed the restrictions would ruin their businesses. To avoid paying the taxes, they disguised their cargoes, landed them at night secretly, or bribed customs officials, who collected the tariffs.

James Otis, a noted Boston lawyer, had helped Adams set up his career as a lawyer in Boston. Boston merchants hired Otis to challenge the right of customs officials to search the colonists' homes for smuggled goods.

James Otis

England's Parliament responded by ordering the court of Massachusetts to give customs officials "writs of assistance." These were general search warrants allowing officials to enter any colonist's home, ship, office, or warehouse to search for smuggled goods.

As Englishmen, the colonists believed they had the right to secure homes without unwarranted searches. They also wanted representatives in Parliament if they were to be taxed. To challenge the writs of assistance, the merchants hired James Otis, one of John's mentors, to argue the case in court. This case was to be the first major clash between the king's government and his subjects in the colonies.

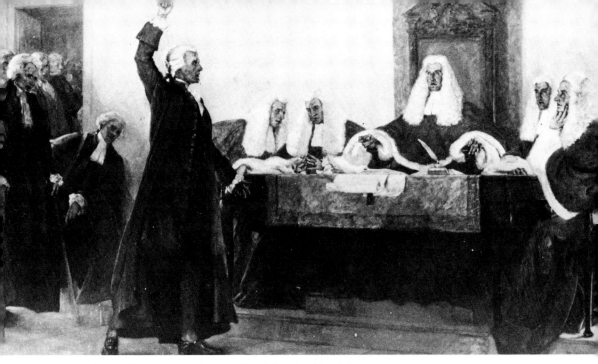

James Otis arguing before Chief Justice Hutchinson

On the court day, John brought quills and a pot of ink to record the arguments in his notebook. He had to shove his way into a seat, as so many merchants and lawyers had come to hear the outcome of the case. Chief Justice Hutchinson and his four associate justices wore their crimson robes and white wigs to emphasize the importance of the trial.

John's other mentor, Jeremiah Gridley, began the legal arguments on the side of the king. He held that history supported the right of Parliament to make laws for the colonies. Otis countered with a brilliant speech that would eventually mold public opinion. During the next five hours he insisted that the writ was against the basic principles of law and man. Colonists would not tolerate high-handed claims from England. ".A man who is quiet and orderly is as secure in his house as a prince in his castle!" Otis insisted.

John welled with excitement. He had long valued "honesty, sincerity, and openness" and believed "men ought . . . to avow their opinions and defend them with boldness." He was so moved he forgot to take notes. Only after he returned to Braintree did he write, "Then and there the child Independence was born!"

Although the case was discontinued and later decided in favor of England, a seed of protest had been planted. Colonists would be split over their differing loyalties. At the time only a few, like Otis and John Adams, thought of a total break with England.

Despite the controls and taxes, America prospered under English rule. Commerce and industry boomed, making Boston a major seaport. The colonial population had grown from 360,000 in 1713 to 1,600,000 in the early 1760s. As part of a vast colonial society, there were schools and colleges teaching science, religion, and classics. There were theaters, concert halls, libraries, dancing, and taverns where men gathered to read and discuss news from London newspapers. Towns were becoming cultural centers, despite their small size.

In May of 1761, Deacon Adams died at the age of seventy after an epidemic of influenza hit Braintree. As a result, John inherited ten acres of farmland near his brothers' shares, a separate twenty-acre farm, and a small house next to the home of his birth. At age twenty-six, John had a growing law practice and owned land. What he craved now was companionship.

One day, John's friend Richard Cranch invited him to visit the Reverend William Smith's house in Weymouth, a

Abigail Adams in
1766 at the age
of twenty-two,
two years after
her marriage to
John Adams

village four miles south of Braintree. Cranch was to marry
Mary, Smith's oldest daughter. Mary had two sisters, Betsy
and Abigail.

John had known Abigail since she was thirteen, when
they met at the home of her grandfather, Colonel Quincy,
a Braintree leader. At those meetings John found her to be
shy. Abigail thought John was stubborn and argumenta-
tive, although she appreciated his fearless, talkative
nature.

Abigail was an odd girl for the times. As a child she had
been too frail to go to school, so her father taught her at
home. Even though it was not fashionable for girls to have
an education, Abigail became an avid reader who buried
herself in the books in her grandfather's library. It was
this keen mind and strong character, coupled with her
graceful dignity and soft brown eyes, that attracted John.

After six months' courting, John asked Mr. Smith for
Abigail's hand in marriage. Abigail's mother had hoped

for a son-in-law from a better family and profession, but she knew better than to oppose her strong-willed daughter. Instead, she stalled the wedding date, saying Abigail was too frail to marry.

Three years later, on October 25, 1764, John was married to Abigail in the parlor of her father's parsonage. Abigail glowed in a red and white woolen dress and a bright new cloak for going away. John wore a white wig tied back from his round face. He dressed in dark blue broadcloth and a white satin waistcoat that his mother had embroidered with gold thread to look like wheat.

Abigail and John rode home on horseback to their house in Braintree near Richard and Mary Cranch's home. Folks thought the Adamses were the perfect couple. Both were from Puritan families with a strong sense of duty, and they shared a deep interest in books and conversation.

Once settled in Braintree, John pursued his law practice in Boston and worked his prospering farm, which was always a joy to him. He began writing humorous essays for the *Boston Gazette* on cultivating crops and livestock, using the name Humphrey Ploughjogger. Any visitor to the Adams home could just as likely find John chopping wood or tossing hay as reading law texts and writing.

John was considered a scholarly young lawyer. In addition, his marriage to Abigail had elevated his social standing to much the same level as his father's. The more wealthy and influential people of Boston sought him out for counsel. Since he was a family man now, he decided to concentrate on his profession rather than on politics — a difficult task, indeed.

Opposite: A 1721 issue of the *Boston Gazette*

 NEW-ENGLAND: N°. 98.

THE
BoſtonGazette

Publiſhed by Authority.

From MONDAY October 2. to MONDAY October 9. 1721.

By His Excellency

SAMUEL SHUTE Eſq;
Captain General and GOVERNOUR in Chief, in and over His Majeſty's Province of the *Maſſachuſetts Bay in New-England,* &c.
A Proclamation for a General

THANKSGIVING.

FOraſmuch as amidſt the various awful Rebukes of Heaven, with which we are frightedſly afflicted, in the Contagious and Mortal Sickneſs among us, eſpecially in the Town of Boſton; The long and immoderate Rains, which have been ſo hurtful to the Husbandry and Fiſhery; And the threatning Aſpect of Affairs with Reſpect to our Frontiers: We are ſtill under the higheſt and moſt indiſpenſible Obligations of Gratitude for the many Inſtances of the Divine Goodneſs in th. Favours vouchſafed to us in the Courſe of the Year paſt, Particularly, For the LIFE of our Gracious Sovereign Lord the KING, Their Royal Highneſſes the Prince and Princeſs of Wales and their Iſſue, and the increaſe of the Royal Family; The Preſervation of His Majeſty's Kingdoms and Dominions from the terrible and deſolating Peſtilence, which hath for ſo long a time been waſting the Kingdom of France; And the happy Succeſs of His Majeſty's Wiſe Counſils for Reſtoring and Confirming the Peace of Europe; For the Continuance of our valuable Privileges, both Civil and Eccleſiaſtical; and the Divine Bleſſing upon this Government in their Adminiſtrations; Particularly, In ſucceeding the Methods taken to prevent the Inſults of the Eaſtern Indians; For giving ſo great a Meaſure of Health within this Province, and Moderating the Mortality of the Small Pox, ſo that a great Number of Perſons are Recovered from that Diſtemper; And for granting us ſo comfortable a former Harveſt, and ſo hopeful a Proſpect of the latter:

I Have therefore thought fit with the Advice of His Majeſty's Council, to Order and Appoint Thurſday the Twenty ſixth Inſtant, to be Obſerved as a Day of Publick THANKSGIVING throughout this Province, ſtrictly forbidding all Servile Labour thereon, and ～～～～ both Miniſters and People in their ～～～～

pective Aſſemblies on the ſaid Day, to offer up humble and ſincere THANKS to Almighty GOD, for His many Favours, as aforeſaid, and for many other Bleſſings beſtowed on a ſinful People.

Given at Boſton, the Eighteenth Day of September, 1721. And in the Eighth Year of the Reign of Our Sovereign Lord GEORGE, by the Grace of GOD of Great Britain, France and Ireland, KING, Defender of the Faith, &c:

By Order of the Governour, with Advice of the Council. S. SHUTE.
J. Willard, Secr.

GOD Save the KING.

The following Advices from Foreign Parts are taken from the Weekly Journal of July 22.

Letters from France ſtill are very full of the Preparations making for the Congreſs of Cambray, and of bringing the long Contention between Spain and the Allies, to a ſpeedy Concluſion. However, notwithſtanding the great Hurry they ſeem juſt now to be in upon this Head, they do not even yet tell us, when this ſo much expected Treaty is to begin, nor let us into the Reaſon for its being delayed; ſo that we are much in the dark about this Affair; and conſidering the uncertain Situation of Things, if we ſhould continue ſo for ſome time longer yet, it would be no manner of Surprize to us.
We can really ſee nothing in our Accounts, that can afford us any Satisfaction as to the Plague in France; for tho' much has been pretended this Week to the contrary, it does not appear to us to have abated any thing of its former Fury, as with much Aſſurance has been given out. If the Voilence of it has been leſs in one Part, it has, as was ſaid in our laſt, been for want of freſh Objects to prey upon; and the Fury with which it has broke out anew, in the Courſe of its dreadful Progreſs, has made it ſufficiently evident, that upon the whole, the Devaſtations continue equally great to what the Diſtemper ever occaſioned ſince it came to its Height. And indeed if we conſider the ſure Footing it has got, the vaſt Number of People and Places infected, and allow the Contagion to be of ſo malignant a Nature as it has all along been repreſented to us, 'twill be much more unexpected, as 'tis really more improbable, to find it abating, and growing leſs, during the violent hot Weather which is now in France, than to hear that it proceeds in the ſame outragous Manner it has already done, till after the Summer Seaſon is over, and the Cold ſets in to check its Advances.

The

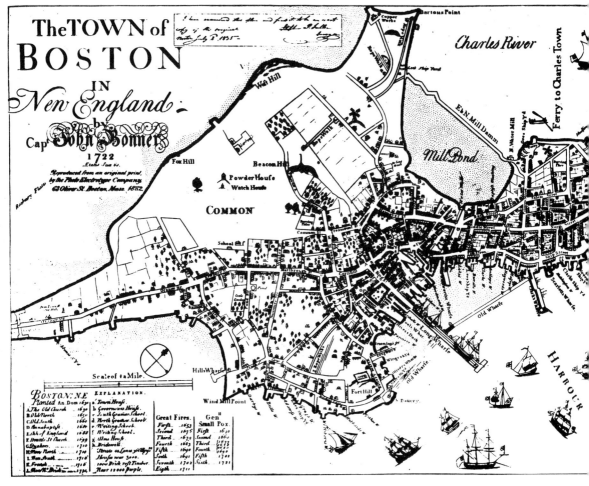

Opposite page—Top: A map of Boston drawn in 1722. Bottom: Boston
Common, a large open field for strolling and, at one time, for grazing cows.
This page—Top: Faneuil Hall (on the right), where many of Boston's
political meetings were held. Bottom: Shipbuilding in east Boston

Angry colonists burning tax stamps as a
public protest against the Stamp Act of 1765

Chapter 5

The Seeds of Rebellion

During their first year of marriage, John and Abigail saw tensions grow between the British Empire and the colonists. When word came that Parliament had passed the Stamp Act in 1765, the colonists were outraged. How could England make them buy royal stamps to attach to every legal document? John would surely lose business. As the word spread in Boston, ships lowered their flags to half-mast and church bells tolled in mourning.

Bostonians organized against the tax. John's cousin, Samuel Adams, united a group of craftspeople and merchants into a revolutionary party called the Sons of Liberty. In August an angry mob ransacked the lieutenant governor's house and burned a stuffed effigy of the stamp distributor from an elm tree in front of the Town House.

Above: The Liberty Tree. Below left: One of the hated tax stamps.
Below right: The sign at The Old Inn in Middleborough, Massachusetts

The tree became known as "Liberty Tree" and was the site of many future protests.

At home, John confided in Abigail, his friend and adviser. He agreed there should be no tax, but he hated mob violence. His method of protest would be through the press.

While Abigail tended their firstborn, a daughter also named Abigail, John wrote a long treatise on English law and oppression that was published in the *Boston Gazette*. In this paper he warned that "British liberties are not the grants of princes or parliaments. . . . Let us dare to speak, that we may be neither led nor driven blindfolded to irretrievable destruction."

Later that year, John wrote more letters to the paper, introducing the concept of "mixed government." His idea was to divide the government into legislative, executive, and judicial branches under a chief executive. Although he was probably not aware of the importance of his ideas at the time, John was laying the groundwork for the United States Constitution.

Meanwhile, John called his Braintree neighbors together to send a message to the Massachusetts legislature that the stamp tax was illegal. While the colonists refused all trade with England, John was becoming known as a spokesman for liberty.

No one but John was surprised when he was called with Otis and Gridley to represent Boston before the king's agents to settle the tax problem. Dressed in a new blue suit with white stockings, John passionately argued against the right of Parliament to tax the colonies.

Though the governor postponed ruling on the case, the colonists' message came through. By now, merchants in England were beginning to suffer from the loss of trade with the colonies. Finally, only a year after it was passed, Parliament repealed the Stamp Act.

A relieved John Adams went back to his law practice, though he kept a close eye on politics. Now with a growing family he needed to make more money. His cousin Samuel suggested that he move to Boston. John agreed that the move would be good for his law practice as well as give him more time with his family.

The move to a white house on Boston's Brattle Square proved beneficial. Although Abigail disliked the noisy, crowded city, she and John enjoyed being together more, watching their new baby, John Quincy, and sharing the happenings of the day. Even more important, John's status improved in the eyes of rural colonists he saw in nearby circuit courts. And Samuel Adams brought him many new clients who supported the cause of the Sons of Liberty. With these clients John formed stronger political ties.

The British governor for Massachusetts thought John could use his skills better if he were working for the crown. So he offered John the position of advocate general in the Court of Admiralty. In this position John would be serving the king's interests in the colonies. At first, John thought of the advantages for his family. But his political views for liberty could not be put aside. No, he would not be bribed.

John resented the offer because of its timing. Parliament had just passed a new set of taxes on imported tea,

Glorious News.

BOSTON, Friday 11 o'Clock, 16th *May* 1766.
THIS Inftant arrived here the Brig Harrifon, belonging to *John Hancock*, Efq; Captain *Shubael Coffin*, in 6 Weeks and 2 Days from LONDON, with important News, as follows.

From the LONDON GAZETTE.

Weftminfter, March 18th, 1766.

This notice was printed and circulated in Boston after the Stamp Act was repealed. The last paragraph announces a "Day for general Rejoicing."

THIS day his Majefty came to the Houfe of Peers, and being in his royal robes feated on the throne with the ufual folemnity, Sir Francis Molineux, Gentleman Ufher of the Black Rod, was fent with a Meffage from his Majefty to the Houfe of Commons, commanding their attendance in the Houfe of Peers. The Commons being come thither accordingly, his Majefty was pleafed to give his royal affent to

An ACT to REPEAL an Act made in the laft Seffion of Parliament, intituled, an Act for granting and applying certain Stamp-Duties and other Duties in the Britifh Colonies and Plantations in America, towards further defraying the expences of defending, protecting and fecuring the fame, and for amending fuch parts of the feveral Acts of Parliament relating to the trade and revenues of the faid Colonies and Plantations, as direct the manner of determining and recovering the penalties and forfeitures therein mentioned.

Alfo ten public bills, and feventeen private ones.

Yefterday there was a meeting of the principal Merchants concerned in the American trade, at the King's Arms tavern in Cornhill, to confider of an Addrefs to his Majefty on the beneficial Repeal of the late Stamp-Act.

Yefterday morning about eleven o'clock a great number of North American Merchants went in their coaches from the King's Arms tavern in Cornhill to the Houfe of Peers, to pay their duty to his Majefty, and to exprefs their fatisfaction at his figning the Bill for Repealing the American Stamp-Act, there was upwards of fifty coaches in the proceffion.

Laft night the faid gentlemen difpatched an exprefs for Falmouth, with fifteen copies of the Act for repealing the Stamp-Act, to be forwarded immediately for New York.

Orders are given for feveral merchantmen in the river to proceed to fea immediately on their refpective voyages to North America, fome of whom have been cleared out fince the firft of November laft.

Yefterday meffengers were difpatched to Birmingham, Sheffield, Manchefter, and all the great manufacturing towns in England, with an account of the final decifion of an auguft affembly relating to the Stamp-Act.

When the KING went to the Houfe of Peers to give the Royal Affent, there was fuch a vaft Concourfe of People, huzzaing, clapping Hands, &c. that it was feveral Hours before His Majefty reached the Houfe.

Immediately on His Majefty's Signing the Royal Affent to the Repeal of the Stamp-Act, the Merchants trading to America difpatched a Veffel which had been in waiting, to put into the firft Port on the Continent with the Account.

There were the greateft Rejoicings poffible in the City of London, by all Ranks of People, on the TOTAL Repeal of the Stamp-Act.—the Ships in the River difplayed all their Colours, Illuminations and Bonfires in many Parts. — In fhort, the Rejoicings were as great as was ever known on any Occafion.

It is faid the Acts of Trade relating to America would be taken under Confideration, and all Grievances removed. The Friends to America are very powerful, and difpofed to affift us to the utmoft of their Ability.

Capt. Blake failed the fame Day with Capt. Coffin, and Capt. Shand a Fortnight before him, both bound to this Port.

It is impoffible to exprefs the Joy the Town is now in, on receiving the above, great, glorious and important NEWS—The Bells in all the Churches were immediately fet a Ringing, and we hear the Day for a general Rejoicing will be the beginning of next Week.

PRINTED for the Benefit of the PUBLIC, by *Drapers, Edes & Gill, Green & Ruffell,* and *Fleets.* The Cuftomers to the Bofton Papers may have the above gratis at their refpective Offices.

The true Sons of Liberty

And Supporters of the Non-Importation

Agreement,

ARE determined to resent any the least Insult or Menace offer'd to any one or more of the several Committees appointed by the Body at Faneuil-Hall, and chastise any one or more of them as they deserve ; and will also support the Printers in any Thing the Committees shall desire them to print.

☞AS a Warning to any one that shall affront as aforesaid, upon sure Information given, one of these Advertisements will be posted up at the Door or Dwelling-House of the Offender.

Left: A notice naming merchants who refused to boycott taxed goods. Above: A handbill warning Bostonians against harassing the Sons of Liberty

lead, glass, and paint called the Townshend Acts. Again, Boston merchants boycotted the taxed goods. John helped Samuel Adams draft a letter to gain support for the boycott. Dispatchers for the Sons of Liberty under the direction of Paul Revere carried the *Circular Letter* to other major seaports in Philadelphia, Pennsylvania, and Charleston, South Carolina. Colonists believed they would soon force this act, too, to be repealed.

But the English were determined that the colonists obey these laws. To enforce tax collection, the crown sent two regiments of troops to Boston Harbor. Angry townspeople refused to house the four thousand redcoats. Most of them camped in Boston Commons, three blocks from the Adams home. All day Abigail and the children heard fifes, drums, and the clumping of heavy boots against the bumpy cobblestone streets.

British troops in Boston

British soldiers fired into a crowd of protestors in the incident known as the Boston Massacre.

The British show of force could not silence the Sons of Liberty or the *Boston Gazette*. Tensions grew between the redcoats and the townspeople. In March of 1770, one month after the death of his third child, Susanna, John heard church bells and saw men running toward the sound. Ringing bells at odd hours usually meant that men were needed to carry water to a burning house, as there was no fire department. But this evening was different.

When John reached the area he found that a small group of British soldiers had fired their muskets into a taunting crowd. Five Bostonians were killed and several others wounded. Captain Preston and six soldiers were arrested.

Samuel Adams demanding that Hutchinson withdraw British troops

Samuel Adams appealed to the governor to remove the British troops, which he did. Next, the accused soldiers were to be tried, but no one would defend them in court. When John was asked to represent those in jail, he agreed. He worried about losing his influence with the Sons of Liberty, but believed that all men should have the right to a lawyer.

At the trial, John questioned ninety-six witnesses before someone came forth to say that the soldiers were forced to fire. In his full white wig and black robe, a heavy and balding Adams pleaded with the jury for mercy. The jury found Captain Preston not guilty and acquitted all but the two soldiers who had exchanged words and shot into the crowd. They were to be branded on the thumb.

AMERICANS!
BEAR IN REMEMBRANCE
The HORRID MASSACRE!
Perpetrated in King-ftreet, BOSTON,
New-England,
On the Evening of March the Fifth, 1770.
When FIVE of your fellow countrymen,
GRAY, MAVERICK, CALDWELL, ATTUCKS,
and CARR,
Lay wallowing in their Gore!
Being bafely, and moft inhumanly
MURDERED!
And SIX others badly WOUNDED!
By a Party of the XXIXth Regiment,
Under the command of Capt. Tho. Preston.
REMEMBER!
That Two of the MURDERERS
Were convicted of MANSLAUGHTER!
By a Jury, of whom I fhall fay
NOTHING,
Branded in the hand!
And difmiffed,
The others were ACQUITTED,
And their Captain PENSIONED!
Alfo,
BEAR IN REMEMBRANCE
That on the 22d Day of February, 1770.
The infamous
EBENEZER RICHARDSON, Informer,
And tool to Minifterial hirelings,
Moft barbaroufly
MURDERED
CHRISTOPHER SEIDER,
An innocent youth!
Of which crime he was found guilty
By his Country
On Friday April 20th, 1770;
But remained Unfentenced
On Saturday the 22d Day of February, 1772.
When the GRAND INQUEST
For Suffolk county,
Were informed, at requeft,
By the Judges of the Superior Court,
That EBENEZER RICHARDSON's Cafe
Then lay before his MAJESTY.
Therefore faid Richardfon
This day, MARCH FIFTH! 1772,
Remains UNHANGED!!!
Let THESE things be told to Pofterity!
And handed down
From Generation to Generation,
'Till Time fhall be no more!
Forever may AMERICA be preferved,
From weak and wicked monarchs,
Tyrannical Minifters,
Abandoned Governors,
Their Underlings and Hirelings!
And may the
Machinations of artful, defigning wretches,
Who would ENSLAVE THIS People,
Come to an end,
Let their NAMES and MEMORIES
Be buried in eternal oblivion,
And the PRESS,
For a SCOURGE to Tyrannical Rulers,
Remain FREE.

Sams. Quincy

John Adams

Samp.ᵉ S Blowers

Left: A handbill describing the Boston
Massacre. The over-dramatic
description shows how outraged the
colonists felt about British
interference in general.
Above: The signatures of all the
lawyers who were involved in the trial
after the Boston Massacre

Samuel Adams and the Sons of Liberty magnified the incident. It became known as the Boston Massacre.

Taking an unpopular case seemed to increase John's popularity as a convincing and able lawyer. He had one of the largest practices of wealthy clients in Boston and was an acknowledged leader in the Boston courts.

Still, John felt disgraced by the trial. With fewer cases and larger fees, John moved his family back to Braintree. Again John spent much of his time away, traveling the circuit courts or practicing in Boston. While he was gone Abigail skillfully handled the farm, the house, and the children, including their fourth child, Charles.

In the fall of 1773, Parliament repealed all taxes except the one on tea. Colonists continued smuggling to avoid the three-penny tax per pound of tea. Without tea trade with America, the British East India Company was close to financial disaster. To save the company, the English government passed a rule allowing the tea to be shipped straight to the colonies. This lowered the cost and saved the company an extra tariff.

But Americans refused to buy tea as long as there was any tax at all. Samuel Adams urged his followers not to let any tea be unloaded in Boston Harbor. If any came ashore, the British would think they had a right to the tea tax.

Samuel Adams kept Massachusetts at the forefront of resistance, and John publicized his ideas. At a meeting of seven thousand townspeople, Samuel announced that the governor planned to fire guns on any ship trying to leave Boston Harbor without unloading its cargo. When the colonists felt they could do no more to resist the oppression, a

group of fifty men and boys disguised as Indians ran to the docks wearing blankets and feathers and shouting war whoops. From three ships they dumped three hundred casks of tea overboard to the sounds of beating drums.

This incident, known as the Boston Tea Party, provoked the British to close Boston Harbor in 1773. There would be no shipping. And this time the Bostonians were forced to house military personnel guarding the harbor. These

Paul Revere (right) was a Boston ironworker, engraver, and artist. He organized horsemen to warn colonists of advancing British troops. This insignia (below) appeared on his shop in Boston. Opposite page: The Boston Tea Party

Paul Revere & Son,

at their *BELL* and *CANNON* Foundery, at the North Part of BOSTON,

measures were thought to be so severe that the colonists called them the Intolerable Acts.

News from Boston spread by Paul Revere's express riders. In an effort to unite all the colonies, Samuel Adams suggested that a congress of delegates meet in Philadelphia.

John approved of the Boston Tea Party, though from a distance. He agreed that "the people should never rise without doing something to be remembered."

Chapter 6

Independence at Last

On August 10, 1774, John Adams, Samuel Adams, and three other Massachusetts representatives left Boston for the First Continental Congress in Philadelphia. They rode in a coach drawn by four horses on one of the few rut-filled roads that linked major cities in the colonies.

Church bells and enthusiastic well-wishers greeted the group along the way. Prominent townspeople came to meet them. On village greens there were cannon salutes, military parades, and feasts. John marveled at the support people showed for struggling Boston.

Continuing south, the travelers found New York to be quite different from Boston. John wrote, "With all the Opulence and Splendor of this City, there is very little good Breeding to be found. . . . They talk very loud, very fast, and all together." John had never been farther from home than Boston. There people were mainly of English Puritan stock. In New York the population of twenty thousand was a mixture of Germans, Irish, Scandinavians, Dutch, and English of every religion.

Opposite: Members of the First Continental Congress
in front of Carpenter's Hall in Philadelphia

Long journeys
in colonial times
were often made
in stagecoaches.
Opposite page:
Public buildings
in Philadelphia
in the late 1700s

After nineteen days of travel, John arrived in Philadelphia dusty and tired. Philadelphia was the leading city in the colonies, with a population of 28,000. Of this city John wrote, "Philadelphia is not Boston . . . we exceed them in every Thing, but in a Markett, and in charitable foundations."

The fifty delegates of the First Continental Congress met at Carpenter's Hall on September 5, 1774. They were the best minds of the time. Some men were wealthy land-owners. Others were tradesmen or lawyers. Many differed on what to do about England. However, everyone agreed that if Boston could be hurt, so could any other town. The meeting gave the colonial leaders a chance to work toward a common goal.

Almost from the beginning, John knew that the power to tax and represent themselves would mean independence for the colonies. But he and the other Massachusetts delegates did not press their views. They wanted to gain support rather than to run the meeting.

The Congress opened with a prayer and then proceeded with the business at hand. From the outset John's legal reputation won him several committee appointments. In committees and as a group, the delegates haggled over what power, if any, to concede to Parliament. John found the progress too slow for his liking.

When the Congress ended on October 28, the group had at least achieved unity of purpose. First, they adopted a declaration of grievances against England and resolved to reconsider the king's latest demands. Second, they petitioned the king for civil rights in the colonies. Third, they created a continental association of representatives from each colony to supervise trade and tighten the ban on English goods.

Back at home again, John tended his farm. The ban had caused a shortage of food and supplies and he needed to work the land for crops. He had done his duty and intended to stay home. He desperately wanted to practice law, but the British occupation kept him from doing so.

Minutemen were called into action at a moment's notice.

When the king received notice from the colonies, he charged they were in open rebellion. More troops were sent to America. John wrote more protests for the *Gazette*.

In every New England town men drilled in readiness. These men were called "minutemen" because they were prepared to act at a minute's notice. Other townspeople cast bullets and stored gunpowder in secret places.

Their chance to fight came on April 19, 1775. A horseman warned John that redcoats were marching to Lexington and Concord, Massachusetts—scarcely twenty miles north of Braintree—where guns and powder were stored.

Paul Revere warning Concord residents that the British are coming

Bells rang, drums rolled, and minutemen headed north. Paul Revere and his riders hurried to warn Concord.

John and his son John Quincy fixed beds of hay for the travelers. Abigail and her maid prepared bowls of porridge and mugs of coffee.

When the fighting was over at Concord, eight townspeople were dead. In Lexington, farmers, minutemen, and townspeople from surrounding villages met the British troops and pushed them back. After hearing news of the fighting, John prepared for a long ride to Philadelphia. Congress would reconvene.

The Battle of Lexington started the American Revolution.

John's eagerness for a separate government classified him as an extremist. Several influential members of Congress, though, were not convinced they wanted independence. As late as January 1776, George Washington's officers drank a toast to the health of the king.

But John was a strong force at the Congress. He worked relentlessly. From seven in the morning to ten in the evening he met in committees or with Congress. As his influence grew he chaired twenty-five committees and served on many more.

The continued fighting showed John that the colonies desperately needed an army and navy to withstand British attacks. The patriots who came to defend Boston had little organization and few supplies. They depended on local farmers for food and lived in tents.

John Adams proposes George Washington as commander-in-chief of the Continental army.

To avoid petty jealousies between the colonies, John suggested George Washington as commander-in-chief of the army. Washington had experience and was a southerner. With him in command, no one could accuse New Englanders in the north of running the Congress.

As public opinion grew for separation from England, delegates became painfully aware of the need for a permanent central government. Congress would have to create a government that could recruit soldiers, levy taxes, and deal independently with foreign powers. John labored long hours writing his *Thoughts on Government*, detailing a plan for state governments with three branches, the executive and legislative branches being elected by the people.

On June 7, Richard Henry Lee made the formal proposal for independence long awaited by John. After its

The committee appointed to write the Declaration of Independence

passage, a committee composed of John Adams, Thomas Jefferson, Benjamin Franklin, Roger Sherman, and Robert Livingston was named to write a formal declaration. The committee chose John and Thomas Jefferson to make a draft. But John preferred that Jefferson write the document. He was a Virginian and a better writer. Also, John said, "I am obnoxious, suspected, and unpopular. You are otherwise." John thought a draft signed with his name would be locked in revision for months.

The Declaration of Independence was officially adopted July 4, 1776. On July 18, it was read in churches throughout the colonies. Afterwards, bells rang, soldiers fired gun salutes, cannons boomed from ships, and all symbols of the crown were destroyed. The Second Continental Congress had laid the groundwork for a new nation.

In CONGRESS, July 4, 1776

The unanimous Declaration of the thirteen united States of America,

When in the Course of human events it becomes necessary for one people to dissolve the political bands which have connected them with another, and to assume among the powers of the earth, the separate and equal station to which the Laws of Nature and of Nature's God entitle them, a decent respect to the opinions of mankind requires that they should declare the causes which impel them to the separation. — We hold these truths to be self-evident, that all men are created equal, that they are endowed by their Creator with certain unalienable Rights, that among these are Life, Liberty and the pursuit of Happiness. — That to secure these rights, Governments are instituted among Men, deriving their just powers from the consent of the governed, — That whenever any Form of Government becomes destructive of these ends, it is the Right of the People to alter or to abolish it, and to institute new Government, laying its foundation on such principles and organizing its powers in such form, as to them shall seem most likely to effect their Safety and Happiness. Prudence, indeed, will dictate that Governments long established should not be changed for light and transient causes; and accordingly all experience hath shewn, that mankind are more disposed to suffer, while evils are sufferable, than to right themselves by abolishing the forms to which they are accustomed. But when a long train of abuses and usurpations, pursuing invariably the same Object evinces a design to reduce them under absolute Despotism, it is their right, it is their duty, to throw off such Government, and to provide new Guards for their future security. — Such has been the patient sufferance of these Colonies; and such is now the necessity which constrains them to alter their former Systems of Government. The history of the present King of Great Britain is a history of repeated injuries and usurpations, all having in direct object the establishment of an absolute Tyranny over these States. To prove this, let Facts be submitted to a candid world.

He has refused his Assent to Laws, the most wholesome and necessary for the public good.

He has forbidden his Governors to pass Laws of immediate and pressing importance, unless suspended in their operation till his Assent should be obtained; and when so suspended, he has utterly neglected to attend to them.

He has refused to pass other Laws for the accommodation of large districts of people, unless those people would relinquish the right of Representation in the Legislature, a right inestimable to them and formidable to tyrants only.

He has called together legislative bodies at places unusual, uncomfortable, and distant from the depository of their public Records, for the sole purpose of fatiguing them into compliance with his measures.

He has dissolved Representative Houses repeatedly, for opposing with manly firmness his invasions on the rights of the people.

He has refused for a long time, after such dissolutions, to cause others to be elected; whereby the Legislative powers, incapable of Annihilation, have returned to the People at large for their exercise; the State remaining in the mean time exposed to all the dangers of invasion from without, and convulsions within.

He has endeavoured to prevent the population of these States; for that purpose obstructing the Laws for Naturalization of Foreigners; refusing to pass others to encourage their migrations hither, and raising the conditions of new Appropriations of Lands.

He has obstructed the Administration of Justice, by refusing his Assent to Laws for establishing Judiciary powers.

He has made Judges dependent on his Will alone, for the tenure of their offices, and the amount and payment of their salaries.

He has erected a multitude of New Offices, and sent hither swarms of Officers to harass our people, and eat out their substance.

He has kept among us, in times of peace, Standing Armies without the Consent of our legislatures.

He has affected to render the Military independent of and superior to the Civil power.

He has combined with others to subject us to a jurisdiction foreign to our constitution, and unacknowledged by our laws; giving his Assent to their Acts of pretended Legislation:

For Quartering large bodies of armed troops among us:

For protecting them, by a mock Trial, from punishment for any Murders which they should commit on the Inhabitants of these States:

For cutting off our Trade with all parts of the world:

For imposing Taxes on us without our Consent:

For depriving us in many cases, of the benefits of Trial by Jury:

For transporting us beyond Seas to be tried for pretended offences:

For abolishing the free System of English Laws in a neighbouring Province, establishing therein an Arbitrary government, and enlarging its Boundaries so as to render it at once an example and fit instrument for introducing the same absolute rule into these Colonies:

For taking away our Charters, abolishing our most valuable Laws, and altering fundamentally the Forms of our Governments:

For suspending our own Legislatures, and declaring themselves invested with power to legislate for us in all cases whatsoever.

He has abdicated Government here, by declaring us out of his Protection and waging War against us.

He has plundered our seas, ravaged our Coasts, burnt our towns, and destroyed the lives of our people.

He is at this time transporting large Armies of foreign Mercenaries to compleat the works of death, desolation and tyranny, already begun with circumstances of Cruelty & perfidy scarcely paralleled in the most barbarous ages, and totally unworthy the Head of a civilized nation.

He has constrained our fellow Citizens taken Captive on the high Seas to bear Arms against their Country, to become the executioners of their friends and Brethren, or to fall themselves by their Hands.

He has excited domestic insurrections amongst us, and has endeavoured to bring on the inhabitants of our frontiers, the merciless Indian Savages, whose known rule of warfare, is an undistinguished destruction of all ages, sexes and conditions.

In every stage of these Oppressions We have Petitioned for Redress in the most humble terms: Our repeated Petitions have been answered only by repeated injury. A Prince whose character is thus marked by every act which may define a Tyrant, is unfit to be the ruler of a free people.

Nor have We been wanting in attentions to our British brethren. We have warned them from time to time of attempts by their legislature to extend an unwarrantable jurisdiction over us. We have reminded them of the circumstances of our emigration and settlement here. We have appealed to their native justice and magnanimity, and we have conjured them by the ties of our common kindred to disavow these usurpations, which would inevitably interrupt our connections and correspondence. They too have been deaf to the voice of justice and of consanguinity. We must, therefore, acquiesce in the necessity, which denounces our Separation, and hold them, as we hold the rest of mankind, Enemies in War, in Peace Friends.

We, therefore, the Representatives of the united States of America, in General Congress, Assembled, appealing to the Supreme Judge of the world for the rectitude of our intentions, do, in the Name, and by Authority of the good People of these Colonies, solemnly publish and declare, That these United Colonies are, and of Right ought to be Free and Independent States; that they are Absolved from all Allegiance to the British Crown, and that all political connection between them and the State of Great Britain, is and ought to be totally dissolved; and that as Free and Independent States, they have full Power to levy War, conclude Peace, contract Alliances, establish Commerce, and to do all other Acts and Things which Independent States may of right do. — And for the support of this Declaration, with a firm reliance on the protection of divine Providence, we mutually pledge to each other our Lives, our Fortunes and our sacred Honor.

John Hancock

Button Gwinnett
Lyman Hall
Geo Walton.

Wm Hooper
Joseph Hewes
John Penn

Edward Rutledge.
Thos Heyward Junr.
Thomas Lynch Junr.
Arthur Middleton

Samuel Chase
Wm Paca
Thos Stone
Charles Carroll of Carrollton

George Wythe
Richard Henry Lee
Th Jefferson
Benja Harrison
Thos Nelson jr.
Francis Lightfoot Lee
Carter Braxton

Robt Morris
Benjamin Rush
Benja Franklin
John Morton
Geo Clymer
Jas Smith
Geo Taylor
James Wilson
Geo Ross
Caesar Rodney
Geo Read
Tho M:Kean

Wm Floyd
Phil. Livingston
Frans Lewis
Lewis Morris
Richd Stockton
Jno Witherspoon
Fras Hopkinson
John Hart
Abra Clark

Josiah Bartlett
Wm Whipple
Saml Adams
John Adams
Robt Treat Paine
Elbridge Gerry
Step Hopkins
William Ellery
Roger Sherman
Saml Huntington
Wm Williams
Oliver Wolcott
Matthew Thornton

The Declaration of Independence, with signatures of members of the Second Continental Congress

Chapter 7

A Decade of Foreign Service

By November 1777, John was hoping to retire from politics. He had been in Congress four years. His farm and law practice were losing money. The children, including his youngest, Thomas, were growing up without him.

But just weeks after returning home, John received word by express rider that Congress had appointed him to join Benjamin Franklin and Arthur Lee in Paris to work on a treaty of alliance with France. He was torn between his desire for privacy and his duty to serve his country. How could he bear another long separation from Abigail and the children?

Of course, Abigail said, he must go. The family would stay behind. The trip was too dangerous and Congress allotted little money. On February 3, 1778, John sailed with his son John Quincy, then ten years old.

After two months of British blockades and rough seas, they reached Bordeaux, France. On the road to Paris John regarded the French countryside as scenic, the wine plentiful, the women brazen, and the religious life horrifying.

Opposite: John Adams, first ambassador to the
English court, is presented to George III.

Once in Paris, he discovered that the business of the American representatives in France was in disarray. The commissioners kept no account books and were spending too much money on too little diplomacy. Shortly after John's arrival, France—and later Spain—declared war on England, adding to the confusion.

John remained in Paris long enough to bring order to the commission. France had helped the colonies repel the British throughout the American Revolution. However, the French government was not willing to recognize the new nation. In frustration, John wrote to request permission to come home. He felt that he didn't fit in with the French, that he was too straightforward and headstrong to be a diplomat, and that three commissioners were too many for one country.

John arrived home after a year and a half, in time to be elected as Braintree's delegate to the Massachusetts constitutional convention. After helping draft the new state's constitution, John was again ready to take up his law practice. Being a diplomat was not for him.

But Congress had different plans. Three months later, in February 1780, John was sent back to France. Congress hoped that England would soon be ready to make peace with America, and that John could help negotiate this peace. Fighting had moved to the southern states. Reports of military successes were mixed. However, reports from London suggested the British people were tiring of war.

Prospects for peace dimmed as John passed three lonely, frustrating years in Paris. The French minister, Charles Vergennes, wanted all peace and trade treaties to be

John Adams as he looked when he lived in Holland

arranged through him. When John clashed with him, Vergennes delayed John's official recognition as a negotiator. While waiting, John wrote articles on the United States' position.

John questioned Vergennes's motives. Not wanting to become too dependent upon France, John went to Holland to seek a badly-needed loan for Congress. His sons John Quincy and Charles, whom John had enrolled in French schools, came to Holland too, and entered the Latin School in Amsterdam.

From Holland John scored a triumph in negotiations. His skill provided a springboard for the Paris treaty that laid the foundation for peace and ended the war. After pushing for the United States to be recognized as a country, John received formal minister status and a loan from Dutch bankers.

D Hartley

John Adams

B Franklin

John Jay ——

Meanwhile, George Washington's troops overpowered the British army at Yorktown. The fighting was almost over, and Vergennes recalled John to France. After many long sessions in Paris, Adams, Franklin, and John Jay signed a treaty of peace with two British commissioners on September 3, 1783.

Now John dreamed of smelling apple blossoms in Braintree and seeing his wife and his other children. Instead, he received a commission to negotiate commercial treaties with twenty European states, including England.

Feeling lonely and worn, John wrote Abigail to bring their daughter Abigail, now eighteen, and be with him. John Quincy, now sixteen and private secretary to the minister to Russia, would join them. They would be reunited for the first time in five years. Unworldly Abigail worried that she would disgrace John by not fitting in, but she came just the same.

The Adams family lived in Auteuil, France, for eight months before John received his appointment as the first American minister to Great Britain. As he left for London, he said, "It was a great thing to be the first American representative of the country you sprung from."

King George III met with John at St. James's Palace in London. John felt he was received politely, considering the awkward circumstances. This was the first time the king had to receive an agent from one of his former colonies as an equal. Afterwards, John said that both men were moved by the meeting.

Abigail and daughter Abby did not fare so well with their invitation to visit Queen Charlotte. The queen kept them waiting almost two hours and was unfriendly. Abigail vowed never again to visit the queen.

John and his family lived in London for three years. During that time John worked to develop good relations between England and the United States. Although he succeeded, he didn't achieve all he wanted. Britain still held some western territories, and America had war debts to settle. A frustrated Adams continued to write papers on government. These papers influenced the framing of the United States Constitution.

In 1788, John realized he had accomplished little in his post and resigned. However, through his appointments and writings, he was establishing himself as the "Father of American Political Science."

Views of Washington, D.C., in 1800

Chapter 8

Mr. President

In the decade when John was out of the country, much had changed. The United States population had increased to almost four million, and postwar business was booming. Slavery had been abolished in the northern states of Connecticut, Rhode Island, and Massachusetts, and conservative Boston now allowed plays to be performed.

More important, the Constitution was written and a new government formed. Throughout the colonies, citizens embraced the Declaration of Independence. Privately, few leaders, including John, believed in equality for *all* the people. Money, talent, and social class still ranked high.

After eight years of fighting to become equal, many people were disillusioned to find that their situations had not changed. For example, the Massachusetts constitution adopted rules for property owners that were twice as rigid as those under British rule. This meant that fewer people could vote. Presently, there was a growing rift between the property owners who could vote and the common folk who were denied the vote.

George Washington is inaugurated as first president of the United States. John Adams stands next to him.

The first business of government after each state ratified the Constitution was to choose a president and vice-president. No one doubted that George Washington should lead the United States, as he had led the country to military victory. It was also agreed that since Washington was a southerner, a New Englander should be chosen for vice-president.

Adams was the natural choice as one of the founding fathers. However, men like young Alexander Hamilton thought him to be too vain and hot-tempered. Hamilton finally agreed to Adams being vice-president, but he conspired so that John won by a small margin.

According to the original Constitution, the winners of the election were the two who received the most electoral votes. Each of sixty-nine electors was to vote for two men.

Crowds of Americans celebrating George Washington's inauguration

Washington received a full sixty-nine electoral votes, the only president to be elected unanimously. John had only thirty-four votes. In addition, Jefferson would be secretary of state, Hamilton secretary of the treasury, and Jay chief justice.

John's vanity was hurt. He had never liked second place. Moreover, he thought Washington was a military hero and not a statesman. He wanted to resign but tried not to let his pride hamper his sense of duty.

On April 30, 1789, less than a year after his return from Europe, John was sworn in as the first vice-president of the United States. Swarms of visitors overran New York City, the first seat of government, to celebrate the event. So many people crowded the taverns and boardinghouses that tents had to be pitched in city streets.

The Adamses' home at Richmond Hill

John and Abigail moved into a manor house at Richmond Hill, a mile and a half outside New York, overlooking the Hudson River. They enjoyed being close to their children again. Charles and Thomas lived with their parents. Abby, her husband William, and their baby lived in New York, and John Quincy was practicing law in Boston.

Abigail eagerly assumed her role as wife of a vice-president. But soon the repetition of the job moved her to write to her sister: "There is so little variety that one letter only might contain the whole History. For Instance, on Monday Evenings Mrs. Adams Receives company . . . as many as curiosity or Fashion tempts, come out to make their Bow or Curtzy, take coffee and Tea, chat a half hour, or longer, and then return to Town again. On Tuesday, the same Ceremony is performed at Lady Temple's, on Wednesday at Mrs. Knox's, on Thursday at Mrs. Jays and on Fryday at Mrs. Washingtons."

John took his job very seriously, aware that his every move would set the custom for years to come. He was so concerned about formal appearances that he was jokingly called "His Rotundity." John felt underrated. Of his office he wrote, "My country has in its wisdom contrived for me the most insignificant office that [was] ever the invention of man."

Meanwhile, John presided over the Senate. Under the Constitution his job was to cast the deciding vote in case of a tie. Although he was supposed to be impartial, his votes leaned toward a strong federal government, rather than toward states' rights. During this first term of the Senate, John cast the most deciding votes of any vice-president in U.S. history.

From 1793 to 1797, Washington and Adams served a second term. The government moved from New York to Philadelphia, where it would stay for the next ten years. A new capital was being built out of the swamps along the Potomac River. Philadelphia teemed with people of every ethnic background. With a variety of businesses, such as tanning, shipping, and metalworking, the city hardly noticed the workings of government.

In the meantime, the public demanded simpler living conditions for their public officials. John received a low $5,000-a-year salary without living expenses. Washington was finding it hard to entertain in the manner of a president on a $25,000-a-year salary. Many of Washington's ablest cabinet members (advisers) resigned because they couldn't afford public life. More and more, Washington relied on Alexander Hamilton, his secretary of the treasury, for counsel. To economize, Abigail returned to Braintree.

Washington's first administration had been calm. But during the second term, war in Europe following the French Revolution was affecting the United States on land and sea. The Spanish, who didn't want America to expand westward, persuaded Indian tribes in the south and west to oppose U.S. interests. The British, who never had left their western posts as agreed to in the Treaty of Paris, stirred up other tribes against the settlers. Both Spain and England were at war with France.

Washington kept strict neutrality. The next president would find peace more of a challenge. Washington refused to serve a third term and retired to his Mount Vernon farm.

By the next election, two political parties had emerged, the Federalists and the Republicans. The Federalists chose Adams as their candidate for president and Thomas Pinckney of South Carolina for vice-president. Hamilton wanted an office but was thought to be too unpopular. Republican Thomas Jefferson ran for president with Aaron Burr of New York as his running mate.

Candidates did not campaign as they do today, but their followers hurled accusations for them. Republican newspapers branded Adams a monarchist for opposing the French Revolution and for imposing formality on the Senate. Federalists charged Jefferson with being a radical for supporting the French Revolution.

A political cartoon knocking Thomas Jefferson's support of the French Revolution

When the electoral votes were counted, Adams received 71, Jefferson 68, Pinckney 59, and Burr 30. This was the only time in history that America had a president from one party and a vice-president from another.

On March 4, 1797, Adams took the oath of office at Congress Hall in Philadelphia. Only five feet, seven inches tall, he looked regal in a gray broadcloth suit with sword attached by a waistband and with a cockade on his hat. Although John made a moving speech summarizing his views on government, it was Washington, the outgoing president, whom the visitors had come to applaud.

John wished Abigail were with him for support. But she had to stay in Braintree to nurse his sick mother. He lived alone in Philadelphia in the three-story house Congress had bought for the president.

An American seaman being forced aboard a foreign ship

Foreign affairs dominated Adams's presidency. War between France and England continued. France was a constant menace to the United States, seizing American seamen, refusing American diplomats, and demanding bribes.

To complicate matters, John was unpopular with his Federalist party. He made appointments based only on merit, rather than on party membership. Furthermore, custom had not yet dictated a change of cabinet with each president. Those loyal to Washington still supported Hamilton, Washington's chief adviser and Adams's enemy. Not wanting to anger the party more, John did not ask for the cabinet members' resignations at first.

American ships were plagued by attacks from French vessels.

Hamilton conspired at every turn to hinder John's peace efforts with France. To make matters worse, John spent much of his presidency in Braintree, as Washington had stayed at Mount Vernon. His orders were often left unattended. It took a while for John to realize Hamilton was running his cabinet.

When Adams acted to make a treaty with France without consulting the party, Hamilton secretly wrote to the Federalists. He said that Adams was unfit for his job and that the government would fall under his direction. As a result, Federalist votes in the 1800 election were split between Adams and Charles Pinckney, giving Republicans the edge. Thomas Jefferson and Aaron Burr received the most votes as president and vice-president. Hamilton's interference had brought about the Federalist party's downfall and cost John a second term.

The campaign had been a long and bitter one for John. Differing opinions caused a final break in relations with Jefferson, his longtime friend. His own party as well as the Republican press attacked him. Although he was a healthy sixty-five years old at the time, newspapers called him "old, querulous, bald, blind, crippled, toothless Adams."

Still, John was proud to have made the first lasting agreement with a European power since the birth of his country. And he was proud to have kept America out of a war with France in spite of his ruthless and powerful opponents.

John moved to the new capital of Washington, D.C., in November of 1800, just before the death of his son Charles. When Abigail joined John in the official President's House, later called the White House, she found it to be a "large and uncompleted castle" in the midst of an almost barren swamp surrounded by forests. Pennsylvania Avenue, the main road connecting the house with the unfinished Capitol a mile and a half away, was muddy brush. Abigail wrote that the house was "upon a grand and superb scale, requiring thirty servants to attend and . . . perform the ordinary business of the house and stables; an establishment very ill proportioned to the President's salary."

The outside of the house was complete, but the inside lacked facilities such as water, staircases, candles for lights, bells to call servants, and enough firewood to heat the rooms still wet with plaster. Abigail marveled that there were trees all around but no help to chop them for firewood.

George Washington observing the construction of the White House

The Adamses held their only reception in the White House Oval Room on New Year's Day, 1801. Wearing a velvet and brocade dress, Abigail was a grand hostess as always. John took his place next to her in the receiving line wearing a black velvet jacket, knee breeches over silk stockings, and silver buckled shoes. Musicians played as guests enjoyed tea, punch, wine, and tarts.

On the eve of Jefferson's inauguration, Adams spent the night signing papers and making last-minute appointments. With a Republican in office, John doubted the Constitution would survive. In hopes of upholding its meaning John chose a strict Federalist, John Marshall, to be chief justice.

On Jefferson's inauguration day John ordered a coach and left Washington without a word. He would be the only president to refuse to greet his successor at the formal inauguration proceedings.

Chapter 9

Retirement to Peacefield

At age sixty-five, an embittered Adams retired from public affairs. After living in Paris, Amsterdam, London, New York, Philadelphia, and Washington, he and Abigail were finally free to live the rest of their lives where they always wanted to be—in Braintree.

With his wife of thirty-seven years, John returned to the house north of Braintree that they had bought upon returning from Europe. The area was called Quincy now, after Abigail's grandfather. John added a new wing to the large house and named it Peacefield in honor of the peace he had made with France.

The Adamses had pleasant days in Quincy. Together they happily worked the farm and made a good living. Although John's Federalist party ignored him, the people of Quincy treated him and his family royally. On Sundays, family, friends, and neighbors gathered at their house after church to pay their respects.

Opposite: The Adams estate in Quincy, Massachusetts

In 1760 and 1761 upon the first Appearance of the Design Of Great Britain to deprive Us of our Liberties by Asserting the Souvereign Athority of Parliament Over Us I took a decided Part against her, and have persevered for Thirty five Years in opposing and resisting to the utmost of my power every Instance of her Injustice, and arbitrary Power towards Us. I am, Sir with much respect your humble Servant John Adams

Above: Part of a letter John Adams wrote in 1815 explaining his political beliefs and actions
Far left: James Monroe, fifth president of the United States
Left: Thomas Jefferson, third president. He and Adams were political allies for a time, political enemies for years, and finally, friends until death.

Although never wealthy, John's family prospered through the years. He had thirteen grandchildren and four great-grandchildren. Of his children, John Quincy would continue in his father's footsteps as a strong public figure. After serving as foreign minister and Massachusetts senator, John Quincy became President James Monroe's secretary of state and eventually president in 1824.

In the early years of his retirement John wrote letters and articles to set history straight about the events of his lifetime. After the death of Thomas Jefferson's daughter Mary, the two men made peace and began corresponding. The exchange was a satisfaction to them both for the rest of their days.

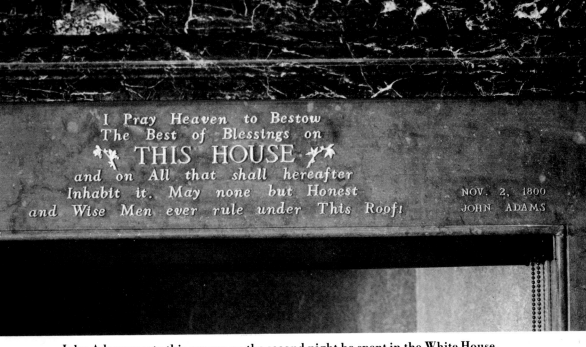

I Pray Heaven to Bestow
The Best of Blessings on
❧ THIS HOUSE ❧
and on All that shall hereafter
Inhabit it. May none but Honest
and Wise Men ever rule under This Roof!

NOV. 2, 1800
JOHN ADAMS

John Adams wrote this prayer on the second night he spent in the White House.

When Abigail died in October 1818—three days after their fifty-fourth wedding anniversary—John was filled with grief. Through the years, Abigail had smoothed his rough edges. Without her constant support, he might not have developed from a small town lawyer to president of the United States. With her behind him, he helped gain independence from England and peace with France. In letters to Jefferson he told how much he missed her.

As John Quincy Adams, the sixth United States president, read the Declaration of Independence on the country's fiftieth birthday—July 4, 1826—his father lay ill in Quincy at the age of ninety-one. The old man opened his eyes to speak for the last time. "Thomas Jefferson survives," he said. But John Adams was wrong. By a twist of fate, Jefferson had died at his Monticello home only a few hours before.

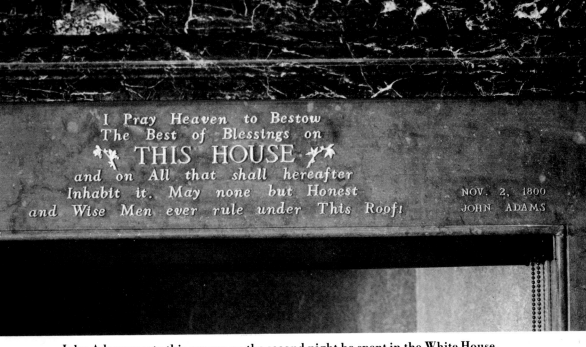

John Adams wrote this prayer on the second night he spent in the White House.

When Abigail died in October 1818—three days after their fifty-fourth wedding anniversary—John was filled with grief. Through the years, Abigail had smoothed his rough edges. Without her constant support, he might not have developed from a small town lawyer to president of the United States. With her behind him, he helped gain independence from England and peace with France. In letters to Jefferson he told how much he missed her.

As John Quincy Adams, the sixth United States president, read the Declaration of Independence on the country's fiftieth birthday—July 4, 1826—his father lay ill in Quincy at the age of ninety-one. The old man opened his eyes to speak for the last time. "Thomas Jefferson survives," he said. But John Adams was wrong. By a twist of fate, Jefferson had died at his Monticello home only a few hours before.

Chronology of American History

(Shaded area covers events in John Adams's lifetime.)

About A.D. 982—Eric the Red, born in Norway, reaches Greenland in one of the first European voyages to North America.

About 985—Eric the Red brings settlers from Iceland to Greenland.

About 1000—Leif Ericson (Eric the Red's son) leads what is thought to be the first European expedition to mainland North America; Leif probably lands in Canada.

1492—Christopher Columbus, hoping to find a sea route from Spain to the Far East, discovers the New World.

1497—John Cabot reaches Canada in the first English voyage to North America.

1513—Ponce de Léon explores Florida in search of the fabled Fountain of Youth.

1519-1521—Hernando Cortés of Spain conquers Mexico.

1534—French explorers led by Jacques Cartier enter the Gulf of St. Lawrence in Canada.

1540—Spanish explorer Francisco Coronado begins exploring the American Southwest, seeking the riches of the mythical Seven Cities of Cibola.

1565—St. Augustine, Florida, the first permanent European town in what is now the United States, is founded by the Spanish.

1607—Jamestown, Virginia, is founded, the first permanent English town in the present-day U.S.

1608—Frenchman Samuel de Champlain founds the village of Quebec, Canada.

1609—Henry Hudson explores the eastern coast of present-day U.S. for the Netherlands; the Dutch then claim parts of New York, New Jersey, Delaware, and Connecticut and name the area New Netherland.

1619—The English colonies' first shipment of black slaves arrives in Jamestown.

1620—English Pilgrims found Massachusetts' first permanent town at Plymouth.

1621—Massachusetts Pilgrims and Indians hold the famous first Thanksgiving feast in colonial America.

1623—Colonization of New Hampshire is begun by the English.

1624—Colonization of present-day New York State is begun by the Dutch at Fort Orange (Albany).

1625—The Dutch start building New Amsterdam (now New York City).

1630—The town of Boston, Massachusetts, is founded by the English Puritans.

1633—Colonization of Connecticut is begun by the English.

1634—Colonization of Maryland is begun by the English.

1636—Harvard, the colonies' first college, is founded in Massachusetts. Rhode Island colonization begins when Englishman Roger Williams founds Providence.

1638—Delaware colonization begins when Swedish people build Fort Christina at present-day Wilmington.

1640—Stephen Daye of Cambridge, Massachusetts prints *The Bay Psalm Book*, the first English-language book published in what is now the U.S.

1643—Swedish settlers begin colonizing Pennsylvania.

About 1650—North Carolina is colonized by Virginia settlers.

1660—New Jersey colonization is begun by the Dutch at present-day Jersey City.

1670 — South Carolina colonization is begun by the English near Charleston.

1673 — Jacques Marquette and Louis Jolliet explore the upper Mississippi River for France.

1682 — Philadelphia, Pennsylvania, is settled. La Salle explores Mississippi River all the way to its mouth in Louisiana and claims the whole Mississippi Valley for France.

1693 — College of William and Mary is founded in Williamsburg, Virginia.

1700 — Colonial population is about 250,000.

1703 — Benjamin Franklin is born in Boston.

1732 — George Washington, first president of the U.S., is born in Westmoreland County, Virginia.

1733 — James Oglethorpe founds Savannah, Georgia; Georgia is established as the thirteenth colony.

1735 — John Adams, second president of the U.S., is born in Braintree, Massachusetts.

1737 — William Byrd founds Richmond, Virginia.

1738 — British troops are sent to Georgia over border dispute with Spain.

1739 — Black insurrection takes place in South Carolina.

1740 — English Parliament passes act allowing naturalization of immigrants to American colonies after seven-year residence.

1743 — Thomas Jefferson, third president of the U.S., is born in Albemarle County, Virginia. Benjamin Franklin retires at age thirty-seven to devote himself to scientific inquiries and public service.

1744 — King George's War begins; France joins war effort against England.

1745 — During King George's War, France raids settlements in Maine and New York.

1747 — Classes begin at Princeton College in New Jersey.

1748 — The Treaty of Aix-la-Chapelle concludes King George's War.

1749 — Parliament legally recognizes slavery in colonies and the inauguration of the plantation system in the South. George Washington becomes the surveyor for Culpepper County in Virginia.

1750 — Thomas Walker passes through and names Cumberland Gap on his way toward Kentucky region. Colonial population is about 1,200,000.

1751 — James Madison, fourth president of the U.S., is born in Port Conway, Virginia. English Parliament passes Currency Act, banning New England colonies from issuing paper money. George Washington travels to Barbados.

1752 — Pennsylvania Hospital, the first general hospital in the colonies, is founded in Philadelphia. Benjamin Franklin uses a kite in a thunderstorm to demonstrate that lightning is a form of electricity.

1753 — George Washington delivers command from Virginia Lieutenant Governor Dinwiddie that the French withdraw from the Ohio River Valley; French disregard the demand. Colonial population is about 1,328,000.

1754 — French and Indian War begins (extends to Europe as the Seven Years' War). Washington surrenders at Fort Necessity.

1755 — French and Indians ambush General Braddock. Washington becomes commander of Virginia troops.

1756 — England declares war on France.

1758 — James Monroe, fifth president of the U.S., is born in Westmoreland County, Virginia.

1759 — Cherokee Indian war begins in southern colonies; hostilities extend to 1761. George Washington marries Martha Dandridge Custis.

1760 — George III becomes king of England. Colonial population is about 1,600,000.

1762 — England declares war on Spain.

1763—Treaty of Paris concludes the French and Indian War and the Seven Years' War. England gains Canada and most other French lands east of the Mississippi River.

1764—British pass the Sugar Act to gain tax money from the colonists. The issue of taxation without representation is first introduced in Boston. John Adams marries Abigail Smith.

1765—Stamp Act goes into effect in the colonies. Business virtually stops as almost all colonists refuse to use the stamps.

1766—British repeal the Stamp Act.

1767—John Quincy Adams, sixth president of the U.S. and son of second president John Adams, is born in Braintree, Massachusetts.

1769—Daniel Boone sights the Kentucky Territory.

1770—In the Boston Massacre, British soldiers kill five colonists and injure six. Townshend Acts are repealed, thus eliminating all duties on imports to the colonies except tea.

1771—Benjamin Franklin begins his autobiography, a work that he will never complete. The North Carolina assembly passes the "Bloody Act," which makes rioters guilty of treason.

1772—Samuel Adams rouses colonists to consider British threats to self-government. Thomas Jefferson marries Martha Wayles Skelton.

1773—English Parliament passes the Tea Act. Colonists dressed as Mohawk Indians board British tea ships and toss 342 casks of tea into the water in what becomes known as the Boston Tea Party.

1774—British close the port of Boston to punish the city for the Boston Tea Party. First Continental Congress convenes in Philadelphia.

1775—American Revolution begins with battles of Lexington and Concord, Massachusetts. Second Continental Congress opens in Philadelphia. George Washington becomes commander-in-chief of the Continental army.

1776—Declaration of Independence is adopted on July 4.

1777—Congress adopts the American flag with thirteen stars and thirteen stripes. John Adams is sent to France to negotiate peace treaty.

1778—France declares war against Great Britain and becomes U.S. ally.

1779—British surrender to Americans at Vincennes. Thomas Jefferson is elected governor of Virginia. James Madison is elected to the Continental Congress.

1780—Benedict Arnold, first American traitor, defects to the British.

1781—Articles of Confederation go into effect. Cornwallis surrenders to George Washington at Yorktown, ending the American Revolution.

1782—American commissioners, including John Adams, sign peace treaty with British in Paris. Thomas Jefferson's wife, Martha, dies.

1785—Congress adopts the dollar as the unit of currency. John Adams is made minister to Great Britain. Thomas Jefferson is appointed minister to France.

1786—Shays' Rebellion begins in Massachusetts.

1787—Constitutional Convention assembles in Philadelphia, with George Washington presiding; U.S. Constitution is adopted. Delaware, New Jersey, and Pennsylvania become states.

1788—Virginia, South Carolina, New York, Connecticut, New Hampshire, Maryland, and Massachusetts become states. U.S. Constitution is ratified. New York City is declared temporary U.S. capital.

1789—Presidential electors elect George Washington and John Adams as first president and vice-president. Thomas Jefferson is appointed secretary of state. North Carolina becomes a state. French Revolution begins.

1790—Supreme Court meets for the first time. Rhode Island becomes a state. First national census in the U.S. counts 3,929,214 persons.

1791—Vermont enters the Union. U.S. Bill of Rights, the first ten amendments to the Constitution, goes into effect. District of Columbia is established.

1792—Thomas Paine publishes *The Rights of Man*. Kentucky becomes a state. Two political parties are formed in the U.S., Federalist and Republican. Washington is elected to a second term, with Adams as vice-president.

1793—War between France and Britain begins; U.S. declares neutrality. Eli Whitney invents the cotton gin; cotton production and slave labor increase in the South.

1794—Eleventh Amendment to the Constitution is passed, limiting federal courts' power. "Whiskey Rebellion" in Pennsylvania protests federal whiskey tax. James Madison marries Dolley Payne Todd.

1795—George Washington signs the Jay Treaty with Great Britain. Treaty of San Lorenzo, between U.S. and Spain, settles Florida boundary and gives U.S. right to navigate the Mississippi.

1796—Tennessee enters the Union. Washington gives his Farewell Address, refusing a third presidential term. John Adams is elected president and Thomas Jefferson vice-president.

1797—Adams recommends defense measures against possible war with France. Napoleon Bonaparte and his army march against Austrians in Italy. U.S. population is about 4,900,000.

1798—Washington is named commander-in-chief of the U.S. army. Department of the Navy is created. Alien and Sedition Acts are passed. Napoleon's troops invade Egypt and Switzerland.

1799—George Washington dies at Mount Vernon. James Monroe is elected governor of Virginia. French Revolution ends. Napoleon becomes ruler of France.

1800—Thomas Jefferson and Aaron Burr tie for president. U.S. capital is moved from Philadelphia to Washington, D.C. The White House is built as presidents' home. Spain returns Louisiana to France.

1801—After thirty-six ballots, House of Representatives elects Thomas Jefferson president, making Burr vice-president. James Madison is named secretary of state.

1802—Congress abolishes excise taxes. U.S. Military Academy is founded at West Point, New York.

1803—Ohio enters the Union. Louisiana Purchase treaty is signed with France, greatly expanding U.S. territory.

1804—Twelfth Amendment to the Constitution rules that president and vice-president be elected separately. Alexander Hamilton is killed by Vice-President Aaron Burr in a duel. Orleans Territory is established. Napoleon crowns himself emperor of France.

1805—Thomas Jefferson begins his second term as president. Lewis and Clark expedition reaches the Pacific Ocean.

1806—Coinage of silver dollars is stopped; resumes in 1836.

1807—Aaron Burr is acquitted in treason trial. Embargo Act closes U.S. ports to trade.

1808—James Madison is elected president. Congress outlaws importing slaves from Africa.

1810—U.S. population is 7,240,000.

1811—General William Henry Harrison defeats Indians at Tippecanoe. James Monroe is named secretary of state.

1812—Louisiana becomes a state. U.S. declares war on Britain (War of 1812). James Madison is reelected president. Napoleon invades Russia.

1813—British forces take Fort Niagara and Buffalo, New York.

1814—Francis Scott Key writes "The Star-Spangled Banner." British troops burn much of Washington, D.C., including the White House. Treaty of Ghent ends War of 1812. James Monroe becomes secretary of war.

1815 — Napoleon meets his final defeat at Battle of Waterloo.

1816 — James Monroe is elected president. Indiana becomes a state.

1817 — Mississippi becomes a state. Construction on Erie Canal begins.

1818 — Illinois enters the Union. The present thirteen-stripe flag is adopted. Border between U.S. and Canada is agreed upon.

1819 — Alabama becomes a state. U.S. purchases Florida from Spain. Thomas Jefferson establishes the University of Virginia.

1820 — James Monroe is reelected. In the Missouri Compromise, Maine enters the Union as a free (non-slave) state.

1821 — Missouri enters the Union as a slave state. Santa Fe Trail opens the American Southwest. Mexico declares independence from Spain. Napoleon Bonaparte dies.

1822 — U.S. recognizes Mexico and Colombia. Liberia in Africa is founded as a home for freed slaves.

1823 — Monroe Doctrine closes North and South America to colonizing or invasion by European powers.

1824 — House of Representatives elects John Quincy Adams president when none of the four candidates wins a majority in national election. Mexico becomes a republic.

1825 — Erie Canal is opened. U.S. population is 11,300,000.

1826 — Thomas Jefferson and John Adams both die on July 4, the fiftieth anniversary of the Declaration of Independence.

1828 — Andrew Jackson is elected president. Tariff of Abominations is passed by Congress, cutting imports.

1829 — James Madison attends Virginia's constitutional convention. Slavery is abolished in Mexico.

1830 — Indian Removal Act to resettle Indians west of the Mississippi is approved.

1831 — James Monroe dies in New York City. Cyrus McCormick develops his reaper.

1832 — Andrew Jackson, nominated by the new Democratic Party, is reelected president.

1833 — Britain abolishes slavery in its colonies.

1835 — Federal government becomes debt-free for the first time.

1836 — Martin Van Buren becomes president. Texas wins independence from Mexico. Arkansas joins the Union. James Madison dies at Montpelier, Virginia.

1837 — Michigan enters the Union. U.S. population is 15,900,000.

1840 — William Henry Harrison is elected president.

1841 — President Harrison dies one month after inauguration. Vice-President John Tyler succeeds him.

1844 — James Knox Polk is elected president. Samuel Morse sends first telegraphic message.

1845 — Texas and Florida become states. Potato famine in Ireland causes massive emigration from Ireland to U.S.

1846 — Iowa enters the Union. War with Mexico begins.

1847 — U.S. captures Mexico City.

1848 — Zachary Taylor becomes president. Treaty of Guadalupe Hidalgo ends Mexico-U.S. war. Wisconsin becomes a state.

1850 — President Taylor dies and Vice-President Millard Fillmore succeeds him. California enters the Union, breaking tie between slave and free states.

1852 — Franklin Pierce is elected president.

1853 — Gadsen Purchase transfers Mexican territory to U.S.

1854 — "War for Bleeding Kansas" is fought between slave and free states.

1855 — Czar Nicholas I of Russia dies, succeeded by Alexander II.

1856 — James Buchanan is elected president. In Massacre of Potawatomi Creek, Kansas-slavers are murdered by free-staters.

1858 — Minnesota enters the Union.

1859 — Oregon becomes a state.

1860 — Abraham Lincoln is elected president; South Carolina secedes from the Union in protest.

1861 — Arkansas, Tennessee, North Carolina, and Virginia secede. Kansas enters the Union as a free state. Civil War begins.

1862 — Union forces capture Fort Henry, Roanoke Island, Fort Donelson, Jacksonville, and New Orleans; Union armies are defeated at the battles of Bull Run and Fredericksburg.

1863 — Lincoln issues Emancipation Proclamation: all slaves held in rebelling territories are declared free. West Virginia becomes a state.

1864 — Abraham Lincoln is reelected. Nevada becomes a state.

1865 — Lincoln is assassinated, succeeded by Andrew Johnson. U.S. Civil War ends on May 26. Thirteenth Amendment abolishes slavery.

1867 — Nebraska becomes a state. U.S. buys Alaska from Russia for $7,200,000. Reconstruction Acts are passed.

1868 — President Johnson is impeached for violating Tenure of Office Act, but is acquitted by Senate. Ulysses S. Grant is elected president. Fourteenth Amendment prohibits voting discrimination.

1870 — Fifteenth Amendment gives blacks the right to vote.

1872 — Grant is reelected over Horace Greeley. General Amnesty Act pardons ex-Confederates.

1876 — Colorado enters the Union. "Custer's last stand": he and his men are massacred by Sioux Indians at Little Big Horn, Montana.

1877 — Rutherford B. Hayes is elected president as all disputed votes are awarded to him.

1880 — James A. Garfield is elected president.

1881 — President Garfield is shot and killed, succeeded by Vice-President Chester A. Arthur.

1882 — U.S. bans Chinese immigration for ten years.

1884 — Grover Cleveland becomes president.

1886 — Statue of Liberty is dedicated.

1888 — Benjamin Harrison is elected president.

1889 — North Dakota, South Dakota, Washington, and Montana become states.

1890 — Idaho and Wyoming become states.

1892 — Grover Cleveland is elected president.

1896 — William McKinley is elected president. Utah becomes a state.

1898 — U.S. declares war on Spain over Cuba.

1899 — Philippines demand independence from U.S.

1900 — McKinley is reelected. Boxer Rebellion against foreigners in China begins.

1901 — McKinley is assassinated by anarchist; he is succeeded by Theodore Roosevelt.

1902 — U.S. acquires perpetual control over Panama Canal.
1903 — Alaskan frontier is settled.

1904—Russian-Japanese War breaks out. Theodore Roosevelt wins presidential election.

1905—Treaty of Portsmouth signed, ending Russian-Japanese War.

1906—U.S. troops occupy Cuba.

1907—President Roosevelt bars all Japanese immigration. Oklahoma enters the Union.

1908—William Howard Taft becomes president.

1909—NAACP is founded under W.E.B. DuBois

1910—China abolishes slavery.

1911—Chinese Revolution begins.

1912—Woodrow Wilson is elected president. Arizona and New Mexico become states.

1913—Federal income tax is introduced in U.S. through the Sixteenth Amendment.

1914—World War I begins.

1915—British liner *Lusitania* is sunk by German submarine.

1916—Wilson is reelected president.

1917—U.S. breaks diplomatic relations with Germany. Czar Nicholas of Russia abdicates as revolution begins. U.S. declares war on Austria-Hungary.

1918—Wilson proclaims "Fourteen Points" as war aims. On November 11, armistice is signed between Allies and Germany.

1919—Eighteenth Amendment prohibits sale and manufacture of intoxicating liquors. Wilson presides over first League of Nations; wins Nobel Peace Prize.

1920—Nineteenth Amendment (women's suffrage) is passed. Warren Harding is elected president.

1921—Adolf Hitler's stormtroopers begin to terrorize political opponents.

1922—Irish Free State is established. Soviet states form USSR. Benito Mussolini forms Fascist government in Italy.

1923—President Harding dies; he is succeeded by Vice-President Calvin Coolidge.

1924—Coolidge is elected president.

1925—Hitler reorganizes Nazi Party and publishes first volume of *Mein Kampf.*

1926—Fascist youth organizations founded in Germany and Italy. Republic of Lebanon proclaimed.

1927—Stalin becomes Soviet dictator. Economic conference in Geneva attended by fifty-two nations.

1928—Herbert Hoover is elected president. U.S. and many other nations sign Kellogg-Briand pacts to outlaw war.

1929—Stock prices in New York crash on "Black Thursday"; the Great Depression begins.

1930—Bank of U.S. and its many branches close (most significant bank failure of the year).

1931—Emigration from U.S. exceeds immigration for first time as Depression deepens.

1932—Franklin D. Roosevelt wins presidential election in a Democratic landslide.

1933—First concentration camps are erected in Germany. U.S. recognizes USSR and resumes trade. Twenty-First Amendment repeals prohibition.

1934—Severe dust storms hit Plains states. President Roosevelt passes U.S. Social Security Act.

1936—Roosevelt is reelected. Spanish Civil War begins. Hitler and Mussolini form Rome-Berlin Axis.

1937—Roosevelt signs Neutrality Act.

1938—Roosevelt sends appeal to Hitler and Mussolini to settle European problems amicably.

1939—Germany takes over Czechoslovakia and invades Poland, starting World War II.

1940 — Roosevelt is reelected for a third term.

1941 — Japan bombs Pearl Harbor, U.S. declares war on Japan. Germany and Italy declare war on U.S.; U.S. then declares war on them.

1942 — Allies agree not to make separate peace treaties with the enemies. U.S. government transfers more than 100,000 Nisei (Japanese-Americans) from west coast to inland concentration camps.

1943 — Allied bombings of Germany begin.

1944 — Roosevelt is reelected for a fourth term. Allied forces invade Normandy on D-Day.

1945 — President Roosevelt dies; he is succeeded by Harry S Truman. Mussolini is killed; Hitler commits suicide. Germany surrenders. U.S. drops atomic bomb on Hiroshima; Japan surrenders: end of World War II.

1946 — U.N. General Assembly holds its first session in London. Peace conference of twenty-one nations is held in Paris.

1947 — Peace treaties are signed in Paris. "Cold War" is in full swing.

1948 — U.S. passes Marshall Plan Act, providing $17 billion in aid for Europe. U.S. recognizes new nation of Israel. India and Pakistan become free of British rule. Truman is elected president.

1949 — Republic of Eire is proclaimed in Dublin. Russia blocks land route access from Western Germany to Berlin; airlift begins. U.S., France, and Britain agree to merge their zones of occupation in West Germany. Apartheid program begins in South Africa.

1950 — Riots in Johannesburg, South Africa, against apartheid. North Korea invades South Korea. U.N. forces land in South Korea and recapture Seoul.

1951 — Twenty-Second Amendment limits president to two terms.

1952 — Dwight D. Eisenhower resigns as supreme commander in Europe and is elected president.

1953 — Stalin dies; struggle for power in Russia follows. The Rosenbergs, first sentenced as spies in 1951, are executed.

1954 — U.S. and Japan sign mutual defense agreement.

1955 — Blacks in Montgomery, Alabama, boycott segregated bus lines.

1956 — Eisenhower is reelected president. Soviet troops march into Hungary.

1957 — U.S. agrees to withdraw ground forces from Japan. Russia launches first satellite, *Sputnik*.

1958 — European Common Market comes into being. Alaska becomes the forty-ninth state. Fidel Castro begins war against Batista government in Cuba.

1959 — Hawaii becomes fiftieth state. Castro becomes premier of Cuba. De Gaulle is proclaimed president of the Fifth Republic of France.

1960 — Historic debates between Senator John F. Kennedy and Vice-President Richard Nixon are televised. Kennedy is elected president. Brezhnev becomes president of USSR.

1961 — Berlin Wall is constructed. Kennedy and Khrushchev confer in Vienna. In Bay of Pigs incident, Cubans trained by CIA attempt to overthrow Castro.

1962 — U.S. military council is established in South Vietnam.

1963 — Riots and beatings by police and whites mark civil rights demonstrations in Birmingham, Alabama; 30,000 troops are called out, Martin Luther King, Jr., is arrested. Freedom marchers descend on Washington, D.C., to demonstrate. President Kennedy is assassinated; Vice-President Lyndon B. Johnson is sworn in as president.

1964 — U.S. aircraft bomb North Vietnam. Johnson is elected president.

1965 — U.S. combat troops arrive in South Vietnam.

1966—International Days of Protest against U.S. policy in Vietnam. National Guard quells race riots in Chicago.

1967—Six-Day War between Israel and Arab nations.

1968—Martin Luther King, Jr., is assassinated in Memphis, Tennessee. Senator Robert Kennedy is assassinated in Los Angeles. Riots and police brutality take place at Democratic National Convention in Chicago. Richard Nixon is elected president. Czechoslovakia is invaded by Soviet and Warsaw Pact troops.

1969—Hundreds of thousands of people in several U.S. cities demonstrate against Vietnam War.

1970—Four Vietnam War protesters are killed by National Guardsmen at Kent State University in Ohio.

1971—Twenty-Sixth Amendment allows eighteen-year-olds to vote.

1972—Nixon visits Communist China; is reelected president in near-record landslide. Watergate affair begins when five men are arrested in the Watergate hotel complex in Washington, D.C. Nixon announces resignations of aides Haldeman, Ehrlichman, and Dean and Attorney General Kleindienst as a result of Watergate-related charges.

1973—Vice-President Spiro Agnew resigns; Gerald Ford is named vice-president. Vietnam peace treaty is formally approved after nineteen months of negotiations.

1974—As a result of Watergate cover-up, impeachment is considered; Nixon resigns and Ford becomes president. Ford pardons Nixon and grants limited amnesty to Vietnam War draft evaders and military deserters.

1975—U.S. civilians are evacuated from Saigon, South Vietnam, as Communist forces complete takeover of South Vietnam.

1976—U.S. celebrates its Bicentennial. James Earl Carter becomes president.

1977—Carter pardons most Vietnam draft evaders, numbering some 10,000.

1980—Ronald Reagan is elected president.

1981—President Reagan is shot in the chest in assassination attempt. Sandra Day O'Connor is appointed first woman justice of the Supreme Court.

1983—U.S. troops invade island of Grenada.

1984—Reagan is reelected president. Democratic candidate Walter Mondale's running mate, Geraldine Ferraro, is the first woman selected for vice-president by a major U.S. political party.

1985—Soviet Communist Party secretary Konstantin Chernenko dies; Mikhail Gorbachev succeeds him. U.S. and Soviet officials discuss arms control in Geneva. Reagan and Gorbachev hold summit conference in Geneva. Racial tensions accelerate in South Africa.

1986—Space shuttle *Challenger* crashes shortly after takeoff; crew of seven dies. U.S. bombs bases in Libya. Corazon Aquino defeats Ferdinand Marcos in Philippine presidential election.

Index

Page numbers in boldface type indicate illustrations.

About the Author

Marlene Targ Brill is a free-lance Chicago-area writer, specializing in fiction and nonfiction books, articles, media, and other educational materials for children. Among her credits are biographical contributions to *World Book Encyclopedia's The President's World* and social studies and science articles for *Encyclopaedia Britannica*. Ms. Brill holds a B.A. in Special Education from the University of Illinois and an M.A. in Early Childhood Education from Roosevelt University. She currently writes for health care, business, and young people's publications, and is active in Chicago Women in Publishing and Independent Writers of Chicago. *Encyclopedia of Presidents: John Adams* is her first book for *Childrens Press*.